## Advance Praise for *A Lens of Love*

"Jonathan L. Walton is one of the very few grand figures in American culture who is both public intellectual and prophetic preacher. His brilliant work and visionary words are legendary at Harvard and throughout the country and the world. This timely book is another testament to his calling, rooted in the legacies of Martin Luther King Jr., Benjamin Elijah Mays, Reinhold Niebuhr, and Fannie Lou Hamer!"

> —Cornel West, Professor of the Practice of
> Public Philosophy, Harvard University

"*A Lens of Love: Reading the Bible in Its World for Our World* excels in bringing together intellectual engagement and a passionate love of God and Scripture. Clearly and beautifully written, it sets a model for how to do biblical theology right—how to come together and reason, how to live faithfully toward justice. It shows how to bring practical theology and social ethics together and inspires its readers to live out a just and faithful Christian identity."

> —Laura S. Nasrallah, Professor of New Testament
> and Early Christianity, Harvard Divinity School

"Springing from the questions, anxieties, and frustrations of the millennials whom he serves, this text gives voice to many of the reasons why people of Christian faith have become either activated or disillusioned by the tyrannies of this moment. Through the powerful narratives of his young constituents and a reclamation of a historical lineage of progressive evangelicalism, Walton contends that the development of a just, contextual, and informed biblical hermeneutic is a critical tool for showing up and speaking up."

> —Neichelle R. Guidry, Dean of Sisters Chapel
> and Director of the WISDOM Center, Spelman
> College, and creator of shepreaches organization

"In a culture of extreme polarization and otherizing, I'm grateful for the voice of Dr. Jonathan L. Walton and his latest book, *A Lens of Love*. In a society that tends to place ourselves—intentionally or unintentionally—in an echo chamber where our assumptions and beliefs are merely affirmed, this book both prophetically and pastorally creates space for the reader to bring their questions and doubts as we engage the Bible. During a time of so much pain, fear, and division, we desperately need to be reminded of God's reconciling truth, grace, and love."

—Eugene Cho, pastor, humanitarian, and author of
*Overrated: Are We More in Love with the Idea of
Changing the World than Actually Changing the World?*

"Love is stronger than death, and this honest, compelling, insightful book on the ethical lens of love by Professor Jonathan L. Walton will resurrect your biblical interpretation. Your ethics of reading Scripture will be guided by a hermeneutic of love. By this approach, Walton stands in a long tradition of biblical interpreters who believe that the rule of love is the greatest rule to follow when reading and living. When you open the pages of this book, you'll feel the love, too, and remember once again that the 'greatest of these' is love."

—Luke A. Powery, Dean of Duke University
Chapel and Associate Professor of Homiletics,
Duke University Divinity School

"A dynamic scholar, passionate teacher, and prophetic preacher, Jonathan L. Walton is one of our most respected and effective leaders in occupying the intersections of biblical and contemporary context and content. We are fortunate to receive his principled voice in the midst of this important moment. As our local and global communities are increasingly connected yet isolated, diverse yet distant, and filled with hope and optimism yet also with panic and aggression, *A Lens of Love: Reading the Bible in Its World for Our World* provides us with a timely trajectory to move us toward matters that matter most. I highly recommend this book for both personal and public study among learners of all ages."

—Brian E. Konkol, Dean of Hendricks Chapel, Syracuse University

"Walton's text is a labor of love. His words sponsor empathy. His erudite, conversational style opens up dialogue about responsible approaches to Scripture. In this current political moment, *A Lens of Love* offers Christian communities a better language by which to engage some of our most pressing social issues."

—Keri Day, Associate Professor of Constructive Theology and African American Religion, Princeton Theological Seminary

"With luminous wisdom and an expansive heart, Jonathan Walton's *A Lens of Love* provides fresh and challenging ways to rediscover the biblical messages of love. These are courageous words of compassionate invitation from a vibrant mind and a loving spirit. Walton gifts us with love-saturated readings that will be ready guides for so many of us seeking hope and possibility in these challenging times."

—David Kyuman Kim, Professor of Religious Studies, Connecticut College

# A Lens of Love

# A Lens of Love

*Reading the Bible in Its World for Our World*

Jonathan L. Walton

WESTMINSTER
JOHN KNOX PRESS
LOUISVILLE · KENTUCKY

*First edition*
Published by Westminster John Knox Press
Louisville, Kentucky

18 19 20 21 22 23 24 25 26 27—10 9 8 7 6 5 4 3 2 1

*Book design by Sharon Adams*
*Cover design by Nita Ybarra*

**Library of Congress Cataloging-in-Publication Data**

Names: Walton, Jonathan L., author.
Title: A lens of love : reading the Bible in its world for our world / Jonathan L. Walton.
Description: Louisville, Kentucky : Westminster John Knox Press, [2018] | Includes bibliographical references and index. |
Identifiers: LCCN 2018007903 (print) | LCCN 2018021808 (ebook) | ISBN 9781611648898 (ebk.) | ISBN 9780664263546 (pbk. : alk. paper)
Subjects: LCSH: Bible--Criticism, interpretation, etc.
Classification: LCC BS511.3 (ebook) | LCC BS511.3 .W355 2018 (print) | DDC 220.6--dc23
LC record available at https://lccn.loc.gov/2018007903

PRINTED IN THE UNITED STATES OF AMERICA

♾ The paper used in this publication meets the minimum requirements of the American National Standard for Information Sciences—Permanence of Paper for Printed Library Materials, ANSI Z39.48-1992.

Most Westminster John Knox Press books are available at special quantity discounts when purchased in bulk by corporations, organizations, and special-interest groups. For more information, please e-mail SpecialSales@wjkbooks.com.

*I dedicate this book to the eldest and youngest living members of my bloodline—the two individuals who bookend my life with faith and promise. They were born at two very different moments into very different circumstances: one on a farm in rural, segregated Dudley, North Carolina, and the other in Cambridge, Massachusetts, on the campus of Harvard University. Beyond blood, it is the acknowledgment of God's love coupled with the powerful stories found in the Bible that will keep their worlds forever united.*

John Curtis Washington (b. May 17, 1924)
Baldwin Cline Walton (b. May 27, 2012)

# Contents

# Acknowledgments

We neither acquire nor expand knowledge in a vacuum. The image of the isolated scholar typing away in seclusion is one that I do not recognize. Hence, there are so many people that I must recognize and acknowledge. I appreciate Don Cutler for listening to my sermons at the Memorial Church of Harvard University and decoding what was, then, my undefined process of biblical interpretation. Young adults encouraged me to start teaching a monthly Bible study and raised the questions that this book seeks to address. Members of the Memorial Church worshiping community including, but not limited to, Diana Rowan Rockefeller, Suzanne and Easley Hamner, Susan Grefe, Robert Maginn, and Laura Malkin provided valuable feedback, critique, and demands for clarity throughout the writing process. And the staff of the Memorial Church, whether on the ministerial, finance, communications, or custodial team, created the conditions for me to dedicate my time to this effort. Thank you for being you, Elizabeth!

No less appreciation goes to my colleagues at Harvard University and members of the Department of Religious Studies at the University of Pennsylvania. I remain amazed at how generous many of my colleagues are with their time and insights. Harvard Divinity professor Laura Nasrallah proved to be my teacher as I sought to find my voice in the fields of biblical and ancient historical studies. She is a rock star! I must also thank the incredible Julie Meadows. Though the scholarly guild knows Dr. Meadows as "The Generous Reader," her frank assessment and critical insights transformed an idea into what I feel now is a readable book. And Professors Justin McDaniel and Anthea Butler, of the University of Pennsylvania, made it possible for me to spend one of the most fruitful and productive years of my life in West Philadelphia. Thanks for the room and hospitality, Professor Shams Inati. You're the best!

The team at Westminster John Knox Press has been nothing short of fabulous. David Dobson is the consummate professional, and Bridgett Green is a great listener, reader, and friend. The brothers at Salem Crossing Barbershop in Lithonia, Georgia, kept my hair tight so that my head could be clear. And my crew of closest friends—you know who you are—Fellas!—kept me laughing when life would say otherwise.

Finally, I need to thank those who suffered and sacrificed most for this book that you hold in your hand. Multiple summers coupled with an academic year away on sabbatical was a lot and, now I unfortunately realize, too much to ask. Thank you, Cecily Cline, Zora Neale, Elijah Mays, and Baldwin Cline for viewing me through the lenses of love and seeing who I strive hard to be, if that is not always consistent with who I am. You deserved better.

Jonathan L. Walton
The Washington Homeplace
Dudley, North Carolina

# PART I

The Promise of Moral Imagination

# 1

## Is There Room? Faith and Intellectual Curiosity

> We must fight their falsehood with our truth, but we must
> also fight the falsehood in our truth.
>
> —H. Richard Niebuhr

> Never speak a word of judgment without first speaking a
> word of grace.
>
> —Emilie Townes

### Questioning Believers

Even for New England, it was an unseasonably cold autumn
evening. Though only October, winter was already in the air.
The transition from fall to winter in Cambridge can be abrupt
and disorienting. Bright colors turn to grey, and beautiful,
casual strolls become harrowing, stressful treks through the
snow. As six young adults sat around my dinner table that night,
I couldn't help but think of the changing outside air as a metaphor for much of what they were feeling inside. As the Plummer Professor of Christian Morals and Pusey Minister in the
Memorial Church at Harvard University, I host such gatherings
with frequency. Typically, my table is full of undergraduates

at Harvard College or older alums who support the Memorial Church financially. On this night, however, it was professionals in their twenties and thirties who live in the Greater Boston area. Their individual lives were changing swiftly. No longer animated by the optimism and innocence of their undergraduate years, many expressed a sense of feeling socially off-kilter, spiritually somewhat askew. Like the incoming cold front, life had come to them fast.

"Is there room for someone like me at this church?" This was the blunt and challenging question Cassie had asked me a few months before when she introduced herself after worship. A research librarian at a local university, she was the group's unofficial spokesperson. Her personality is like the crackling flames that danced in the fireplace next to us. Cassie is warm and engaging but can scorch you with her quick wit and sarcasm—think Ellen DeGeneres with a master's degree in geology.

"Of course," I replied. "There is room for everyone here." Her pursed-lipped expression told me that she was not convinced. I soon discovered that Cassie, whether she realized it or not, was representing a larger group of congregants. This group sits neatly tucked in the middle pews, three-quarters of the way back on Sunday mornings. They rest betwixt and between other constituencies at the Memorial Church. They are far enough removed from the undergraduate experience that student-oriented ministries do not address their concerns. Only a few are married with kids, and thus they do not find community among the church school families. And none has the time, like the local retirees, to start each day at morning prayers, hang out for coffee, or attend the many lectures and cultural events taking place in Cambridge. No, this group is distinct.

They sat down at my table with particular spiritual aspirations as well as personal anxieties. Postadolescent urban existence can be difficult for even the most highly accomplished individuals. Navigating these challenges as people of faith served as the crux of our dinner conversation that night.

The book that you now hold in your hand is the result of this dinner party. What started as an intimate gathering led to a monthly Bible study series at the Memorial Church. These young adults wanted to know the tools and techniques of biblical studies to gain a better understanding of what the Bible is all about. This included understanding more about the world in which the Bible was produced and the major issues the Bible sought to address in the ancient world. Their goal was not just academic. To the contrary, those gathered around my table wanted to know how to apply the teachings of the Bible to wrestle with the big questions of contemporary life. How do we live ethical and just lives as Christians? How do we become deeply rooted in our Christian faith while respecting those who may not look, love, or believe as we do?

Fittingly, the group was racially, regionally, and religiously diverse. Participants had grown up in a range of areas that included Southern California, suburban Atlanta, metropolitan Detroit, and Upstate New York. There were those who identified as Caucasian, Asian American, African American, and Hispanic (nonwhite). And members of the group represented a range of Christian traditions: Catholic, pentecostal, Methodist, Episcopalian, and nondenominational charismatic. Despite such beautiful diversity, our sessions revealed how much they shared in common as people of faith. Each desired a deeper understanding and engagement with the Bible as well as a Bible-based approach to Christian living. Their most shared and recurring goals included:

- attaining an increased level of comfort with the Bible;
- understanding the more problematic dimensions of the Bible, such as its overt sexism and violence and Paul's troubling views on slavery;
- reconciling statements in the Bible with ongoing scientific discoveries that often contradict Scripture; and

- identifying how the Bible can still inform ethical decisions and political choices in a radically different world than the one in which it was produced.

This last stated goal was particularly important for the youngest member at the dinner table, Carlos. Carlos grew up in Miami in a Catholic and Pentecostal household, a very common pairing among Latino families in both the United States and the Global South. He was enrolled in a joint graduate program in law and business, two of the higher-earning fields among the professional schools at Harvard. This is one of the reasons Carlos was so adamant about holding on to his Christian-informed commitments to care for the most vulnerable. He knew that he would be entering fields that, unfortunately too often, are prone to place profits over people and bottom lines over social good. Carlos wanted to know if the Bible has anything to say about unjust structures that are far removed from the worlds of the ancient Near East.

To Carlos, I say with confidence, "Absolutely!" It is just a matter of learning how to read the Bible in its world so that we might apply it to our world. In the pages that follow, I will introduce you to the reading and interpretive strategies that I presented to students in our monthly Bible study class. Most notably, I offer in this book the practical and ethical strategies that I employ when preparing a sermon. As a social ethicist, one who is concerned with cultural values and how societies define the right, the good, and the just, I most often use what is called the sociohistorical approach. This approach to reading pays attention to the social relations and political dynamics within the ancient world. The social and cultural contexts help us to identify power dynamics and class structures, as well as the influence of surrounding cultures such as the Egyptian, Babylonian, and Roman Empires.

Others noted a concern with learning and living into their moral responsibility as Christians. Each expressed an interest in demonstrating their Christian faith in every area of their life. Consider Derrick, a lawyer and aspiring politician, who is deeply committed to social justice issues. Professing a progressive political identity was for him part and parcel of what it meant to model the radically inclusive love of God. He learned this from the African American Protestant churches in his hometown of Detroit. Derrick wanted to better integrate his spirituality into his profession without appearing as if he was wearing his faith on his sleeve. In a world where so many perform their faith for personal and political gain, Derrick wanted to live it naturally. His passion reminded me of the words attributed to the thirteenth-century Catholic friar Francis of Assisi: "Witness always; use words when necessary."

Sitting next to Cassie was Trina, a university program manager. Trina confessed to finding it difficult to date what she described as "normal guys" without concealing her faith. She felt that too many men in her dating pool associated being a practicing Christian with anti-intellectual "holy rollers." Trina had a strong sense that her friends and coworkers believed that so-called organized religion makes a person dogmatic and parochial rather than open and accepting. This is one of the reasons Trina grew up thinking that one's religious faith should be kept private. In the words of the late philosopher Richard Rorty, religion proves to be a "conversation stopper." Add to this mix what Trina described as "some pretty ugly" Catholic and Protestant family feuds among her white, working-class ancestors, and her reluctance to share her faith freely is understandable. Nevertheless, after attending the Memorial Church for a handful of years, Trina now feels that she need not be ashamed of her Christian identity—an identity that she believes makes her more compassionate, kind, and loving to everyone. Her faith is not a small thing. To the contrary, it is germane to her personality and inquisitive approach to the world. This is why she now wants to find ways to show both her friends and potential partners the importance of her Christianity without coming across as defensive.

The group raised several other concerns. Evelyn, a recent

transplant from Southern California, had trouble negotiating what appeared to be the many prohibitions of Christianity. Her older brother had come out as gay a few years before. Evelyn was thus very uncomfortable with how so many Christians, namely, those within the Asian American churches of her youth, treat the topic of same-gender love based on their interpretation of certain biblical texts. Cassie agreed strongly with Evelyn. She added other issues of concern to the discussion, such as the overt sexism and gender hierarchies throughout the Hebrew Bible and New Testament. Each person sitting around the table believed that God's love, coupled with expanded human knowledge in the physical and social sciences, countered some of the more traditional interpretations of Scripture that today's churches still teach. Nobody at dinner felt informed enough about Scripture to make a sound case for their belief.

This was the case for Paul. Paul was completing his final year of medical residency in the Boston area. Born in Atlanta, he had a southern accent and charm that served as a beautiful complement to his Chinese ethnicity. Paul had grown up in a Christian household and even attended the Memorial Church during his years as an undergraduate at Harvard. But he felt woefully unprepared to stand up against his Christian friends who read the Bible more literally than he was comfortable doing. Paul shared with us one instructive example. At one point he was dating someone who attended a conservative evangelical megachurch. "She knew her Bible well," he declared, adding that she did not feel Scripture needs interpretation. Like many self-professed biblical literalists, she believed that the Bible is simple and straightforward. It is just up to us to do what it commands.

Paul knew that such a dogmatic approach to Scripture belies everything he ever learned in college about how a text plus the larger context creates meaning—that is, what we call interpretation. Because Paul felt that his understanding of the Bible was so rudimentary, he did not feel comfortable pressing his friends on statements in the Bible that he was confident were up for ethical, scientific, and interpretive debate. Hence, Paul's interest in developing biblical knowledge is in order to have constructive conversations with people who he felt seem so much more biblically literate than him. Whenever it came to having debates about important moral issues such as racism, homophobia, and poverty, Paul went silent. Such silence, he felt, ultimately betrayed his faith.

It was this sense of silence born of biblical insecurity that became the recurring theme at dinner. I knew exactly where these young people were coming from. Having been raised a progressive evangelical in the southern United States, I understood their frustration. Though I consider myself within a long, productive tradition of evangelicals who fought for progressive social causes such as abolitionism, women's suffrage, and various forms of civil rights, declaring that I am an evangelical Christian at a place like Harvard earns me all kinds of skeptical looks. People have images of Jerry Falwell and the Moral Majority, James Dobson and Focus on the Family, as well as a host of gilded televangelists who preach viewers into hell in the afterlife while trying to untether them from their finances in this life.

It is a shame that more people do not reference progressive evangelicals such as nineteenth-century Presbyterian minister and Oberlin College president Charles Grandison Finney. His evangelicalism encouraged him to promote equal access to higher education for all, regardless of race or gender. Few reference the evangelical roots of abolitionist sisters Sarah and Angelina Grimke or the social gospel theologian Walter Rauschenbusch, whose writings called for the conversion of the individual as well as challenged social structures that led to poverty and disillusionment. And when scholars trace the history of evangelicalism in the twentieth century, rarely do they mention Mary McLeod Bethune, the Methodist educator who organized Bethune-Cookman College, or Benjamin Elijah Mays, the Baptist minister who served as president of Morehouse College over the course of three decades.

Unlike the more referenced evangelists such as Oral Roberts and Billy Graham, both McLeod and Mays served as architects of the civil rights struggle. Unfortunately, by the final quarter of the twentieth century, this rich tradition of biblically engaged, intellectually progressive Christians had been largely erased from the national narrative of what it meant to be a "believer." I use this term intentionally here since it was the term embraced by conservative evangelicals and former segregationists such as Jerry Falwell to forge political alliances with Christian fundamentalists such as Francis Schaeffer, a conservative Presbyterian minister who left the United States for Switzerland, where he started the L'Abri community (French for "shelter"). Whereas the latter withdrew from social engagement for the better part of the previous century, conservative evangelicals remained politically engaged. It was their reunion around the concept of the believer that allowed them to join forces in the final quarter of the twentieth century and form the Religious Right.

"Believer" became a politically loaded term that signified adherence to a theological litmus test that was not much different from the five-point fundamentalism established in 1910 by the Presbyterian General Assembly. Developed in response to concerns about the "orthodoxy" of graduates of Union Theological Seminary, the five points are: (1) universal Christian acceptance of the **inerrancy of Scripture**, (2) the deity of Christ, (3) Christ's virgin birth, (4) the **substitutionary atonement** of Christ, and (5) Jesus' physical resurrection and impending bodily return to earth. By the 1980s, these points came to constitute what it meant to be an evangelical. Therefore, and unfortunately, news media outlets, religious leaders, and even many scholars of religion began to use the term "evangelical" as shorthand for those white, politically conservative Christians who adhered to the five fundamentals of the faith.

This view of the faith erased generations of evangelical social gospelizers, such as one of my predecessors at Harvard, Plummer Professor Francis Greenwood Peabody, as well as the most famous American evangelical of the previous century, Martin Luther King Jr. They are now framed as "liberal Christians," because conservatives effectively laid claim to the categories of "evangelical" and "believers." (Notice how equating the term "believers" with conservative Christians suggests that progressive Christians, Jews, Muslims, or followers of any faith that differs from theirs are somehow "nonbelievers.") Unfortunately, the success of the conservative evangelical media campaign has helped to frame American Christianity by establishing the cultural terms. As in politics, the larger the audience, the more pared down the message must be. We see this dynamic on the radio, on television, and in other forms of advertising. Some refer to it as the KISS principle of communication (Keep It Simple, Stupid!). This helps to explain why so many outside of the faith have accepted the view that Christians are intellectually simplistic. When the most famous preachers and theologians pedal in cliché phrases that resonate with default assumptions about life—for example, "God wants you to be wealthy and blessed" or "God made Adam and Eve, not Adam and Steve"—then scientific discovery and the more complicated realities of life become inconvenient.

In fact, at least half of my dinner guests felt this sort of cultural pressure from more conservative Christians. Since they did not accept so-called biblical literalism like the "believers" they knew, some felt like they were hypocrites. This was the case with Trina. "I have plenty of doubts, questions, and flat-out issues with many things contained in the Bible," she confessed. "And because there are parts of the Bible, and Christian doctrine in general, that I am not fully on board with, I worry that I may actually be one of those hypocrites that I used to assume others to be—those who show up at church every Sunday but who don't actually put any thought into what they are being asked or expected to believe." Trina, like the other dinner guests, felt that the pat, simplified biblical responses to life's complicated questions were insufficient. She needed more. Like the eleventh-century Benedictine monk Anselm of

Canterbury, Trina and others around the table had faith that sought greater understanding.

Such an understanding must take the form of the **sociohistorical approach**, which begins with the belief that there is no text without context. The aim of this approach is to open up the ancient world in which the Bible was produced. For instance, considering the power dynamics between men and women, Israelites and Canaanites, and among Romans and Jews helps to track the lives of biblical characters that Scripture reveals God cares most about—namely, the vulnerable and the violated. Though there may not have been a working class, middle class, and upper class in the ancient world in the way we conceive of them in a contemporary capitalist society, this does not mean that people were not divided along class lines. Social categories such as family lineage, occupation, and even ethnicity placed people on different rungs on the social ladder.

Moreover, it is important to note the role of empire in the ancient world. There is a common saying that history is written by the victors. This is not true of Jewish Scriptures and the writings of the early Jesus movement, even as we acknowledge that those in power employed biblical texts to justify imperial power. But whether those enforcing or resisting power wrote Scripture, the influence of political power always hovered in the background.

Finally, it is important to examine why certain stories became sacred and why particular metaphors were used to describe God more than others. Only when we start to immerse ourselves in the world of the Bible will we have a semblance of understanding of what biblical writers understood themselves as saying. This book makes the argument that to know Scripture is not merely a matter of one's ability to recite verses from memory. Faithful and responsible biblical interpretation searches for possible meanings according to the context in which it was produced. Thus, the better we understand what the ancients were trying to convey about God, power, injustice, evil, suffering, and hope in their world, the better we might be able to make moral connections across space and time in our world.

## A Critical Mind and Sensitive Heart

I am an avid reader of the Bible. This applies to my professional life by necessity. I trained as a social ethicist. My scholarly research focuses on the intersection of religion and advanced media technologies in contemporary society, paying particular attention to Protestant communities and the moral problems they face. The way evangelical Christians conceive of God and the role of the church in society informs their political choices. If someone, for instance, believes God to be the source of all financial wealth and good health, then this will affect how they view governments' role and responsibilities in providing basic goods and social services. Christians always measure their views of contemporary society and political choices against their reading of Scripture. These interpretations serve as the means to legitimate, challenge, or debate the role of religion and culture, as well as faith and politics. Understanding how others read the Bible is necessary for me as a scholar and researcher.

An additional professional reason for the Bible's importance to me is that I am called to provide responsible and accessible interpretations of biblical texts from the pulpit at the Memorial Church of Harvard University. This is a beautiful yet daunting task. Hundreds fill the pews of the Memorial Church every week, with thousands more live streaming the services and downloading sermons from various media platforms. One never knows who is listening, nor their particular need. I thus seek, prayerfully and carefully, to craft sermons that are radically inclusive and theologically expansive for a diverse audience.

My sermons aim for radical inclusion insofar as I attempt to emphasize characters in the Bible who are furthest from the center of power and privilege. I strive to highlight the extensive nature of God's compassion and care. As it is written in the book of Matthew, if God can keep watch over the smallest sparrow, we should have confidence that we, too, fall quickly in God's line of sight (Matt. 6:26; 10:29–31). A theologically expansive sermon is one that demonstrates that there are resources in both the Hebrew Bible and New Testament for all persons regardless of their religious background or faith perspective. Such notions of love, hope, confronting life's disappointments, and challenging injustice is not the exclusive concern of Christians. All who walk in the door of the Memorial Church, no matter their walks of life or faith traditions, want to hear a message that can help them love right and live right.

My particular sermonic approach is rooted in the progressive African American preaching tradition. This tradition takes Scripture very seriously. There is a common refrain in historically black churches that the preacher ought to just "tell the story." So much of what the people need to hear about battling evil and injustice with love and hope is found in the rich stories of the Bible and activated in telling the story again and again.

Consider Martin Luther King's erudite analysis of the injustices associated with segregation in his "Letter from a Birmingham Jail." His ability to cite biblical stories as a way of offering visions of a more just and radically inclusive society is evidence of his high regard for Scripture. Though he references philosophers from Socrates to Aquinas, theologians such as Martin Buber and Paul Tillich, and even the poet John Donne, this letter, like his sermons, always returns to biblical stories and themes. This is a result of the black Protestant evangelical community that produced him. This is the tradition that produced me. The high place of Scripture in this tradition, coupled with a sincere commitment to social justice, demands that the minister lift up the biblical text as a source of both personal comfort and moral challenge.

Though I read the Bible out of professional necessity, my relationship with the Bible began as a personal choice. The Bible remains an integral part of my identity. It represents the power of God and the potential for my life as a person of faith. I grew up in a beautifully enchanted world. As a young child, my parents took me to Clifton United Methodist Church, where I listened to the Rev. Richard Winn make the biblical characters come to life. I learned from David's triumphs and tragic failures as king. Shadrach, Meshach, and Abednego's courage and ultimate deliverance from a fiery furnace continue to come to mind during moments of adversity and challenge. And the apostle Paul, coupled with a loving community of faith, convinced me that I could be more than a conqueror in Christ who loved me (Rom. 8:37). I would go so far as to say that among the many things that my family bequeathed to me, a productive relationship with Scripture is among the gifts I value most.

Even as I write these words at my grandparents' home in North Carolina, my ninety-three-year-old grandfather continues to inspire me with his daily ritual of biblical devotion. A successful newspaperman and community leader in Raleigh, John Curtis Washington spent the first half of his life trapped under what W. E. B. Du Bois called the veil of racial segregation. The Bible has always represented for him the love of God, love of self, and love of humankind. Though some used the Bible to justify Jim Crow, at an early age, he learned to read and interpret the Bible for himself. My grandfather did not have the interpretive techniques or historical insight offered in this book, but he had two things that are essential to responsible biblical interpretation: a critical mind and a sensitive heart. Both are vital for intelligent and faithful readings of the Bible.

### Reading More Yet Learning Less

My grandfather is not alone. Millions of Americans look to the Bible with spiritual longing and aspiration. A recent survey conducted by the Center for the Study of Religion and American Culture at Indiana University–Purdue University Indianapolis (IUPUI) reveals that nearly half of Americans have read parts of the Bible over the past year. People rely on Scripture to make personal decisions, cope with tragedy, strengthen relationships, and find ultimate meaning for their life. Jesus' dealings with those on the margins of society inspire some to be warmer and welcoming to strangers. The poetry of the Psalms offers comfort to grieving families on innumerable occasions. The Bible reminds us that we, too, are characters in the divine story that God continues to coauthor with us.

The findings of the IUPUI study suggest that most readers are taking this particular approach to the Bible. Such an overwhelmingly personal approach to the Bible makes sense to me in our contemporary American context, as a narrative of self-help has remained a powerful cultural current since our nation's founding. From Norman Vincent Peale's *The Power of Positive Thinking* to today's Chicken Soup for the Soul empire, it is easy to get caught up in popular media's persistent call to awaken our inner Tony Robbins or Oprah Winfrey. And while the Bible has always served as a source of help, hope, and healing within communities of faith, the current context of individualism exacerbates this particular reading approach at the expense of all others.

Unfortunately, this also fosters an interpretive problem. If the vast majority of us go to the Bible for individual comfort, asking the question, "What does this text mean for me?" we will end up regarding as superfluous an essential question: "What did this text mean at the time of its composition?" If we start with trying to identify personal meaning, this will only cause us to cherry-pick verses deemed personally therapeutic. The act of biblical interpretation gets reduced to self-help.

If biblical literacy only refers to the capacity to quote Scripture, then this is not necessarily a positive asset to Christian communities. Rote memorization does not contribute to responsible biblical interpretation. Though individual communities may privilege the knowledge of biblical verses, it often means little to the interpretive process. The Bible is best misused and abused by those who know it well! The meaning of Scripture is determined by historical and cultural context, but this is an area that many Bible study groups seem to ignore. So even if all Christians knew the difference between John the Baptist and John the Revelator and can quote John 3:16, that would not automatically translate into biblical literacy.

There is another reason that I believe people opt for the easier route of superficial, selective reading of Scripture. The Bible is intimidating! Sixty-six individual books comprise the Bible. The verbiage is often arcane, and we can spend immense intellectual energy trying to keep track of who begat whom and whether Thou is that which begat Thee! Others have noted that the flow of many texts appears random and haphazard, making it seemingly impossible to follow a narrative arc. There are good reasons for this. The sixty-six books of the Bible were not written with the intent that they be read linearly, beginning with Genesis and ending with Revelation.

Consider the Old Testament, more appropriately known as the Hebrew Bible. It comes across to us as a hodgepodge of stories. To ancient communities, these stories constituted the terms of their society. They were passed down orally from one generation to the next over a thousand years. The context of specific illustrations employed throughout is as foreign to today's readers as a laptop would have been to William Shakespeare or an MP3 player to Ludwig van Beethoven. This may help to explain why, despite our best intentions, so many of us are repeat failures in our attempts to read the Bible. We hear the sermon on Sunday and commit ourselves to picking up that Bible from the shelf, yet before long it is promptly placed back on our nightstand as part of our bedroom's spiritual decor.

## Organization of the Book

This book has two primary tasks. First, by engaging four major sections of the Bible—the Dynastic literature, the Pentateuch, the Gospels, and the Epistles—we will approach the books of the Hebrew Bible and New Testament in digestible and genre-specific clusters. This can help us to wrap our minds around a world that was radically different from our own. The aim here is to understand better how and why the ancients imagined and described God in the way that they did. We will identify metaphors, stories, and symbols of the ancient world commonly associated with the divine.

The Dynastic literature, for instance, provides an account of the rise and fall of Israel's monarchy. We begin here, seemingly in the middle of the Hebrew Bible, because many of the figures and events of this period can be historically verified independently of Scripture. Historians and archaeologists have discovered facts about the Egyptian, Assyrian, Babylonian, and Persian Empires that help us understand better the biblical stories about Israel's monarchy and captivity.

What is more, the Dynastic literature provides the backdrop for the entire Hebrew Bible. It is the context in which most of the texts of the Hebrew Bible were recorded, and the exilic period informs how ancient Israel reconstructed its past and imagined its future. Understanding the social and historical contexts in which the nation was united under one leader, King David, along with its subsequent civil war and split into the northern kingdom of Israel and southern kingdom of Judah, will illumine other aspects of the Hebrew Bible. The Hebrew prophets, the Wisdom literature, and the origin narratives in the Pentateuch all speak to the nation's split in explicit and implicit ways. When we read some of the familiar stories found in the Pentateuch, we will see that many were political allegories to defend, rebuke, or explain the behaviors of individual leaders as well as the nation of Israel during its rise and fall.

We will then turn to the New Testament with the Gospels and writings of Paul. All twenty-seven books of the New Testament hinge on the lives of two primary characters: Jesus of Nazareth and the apostle Paul. The Gospels offer spiritual biographies of Jesus that were in circulation decades after his crucifixion. They also can tell us much more. By reading the

Gospels with an eye to their original context in the Greco-Roman world, we can better interpret the subversive teachings of the Jesus movement and understand and explain ethical debates among Jews in ancient Palestine.

The Epistles speak to the composition and character of early Jesus movement communities, as Paul, a primary organizer of these communities, uses his letters to help organize, encourage, and admonish churches throughout the Roman Empire. These letters also reveal much about the religious controversies, theological questions, and church-related concerns that emerged during the earliest decades of the Jesus movement. Keeping our focus on the Dynastic literature and Pentateuch in the Hebrew Bible, and the Gospels and Epistles in the New Testament, will provide a substantial introduction to the shape, theological content, and genres of writing that constitute the Bible. And while books of the Bible not covered, such as Psalms and Revelation, are essential to spiritual life, for the sake of time and space I have opted to limit my scope so that this book might be more manageable for me as a writer and you as the reader.

The second primary task of this book involves its subtitle: *Reading the Bible in Its World for Our World*. This is a book to promote ethical and responsible biblical interpretation among nonspecialists. To live a life that is consistent with the love and grace of God as recorded in the Bible means that we must wrestle with Scripture, including difficult passages. Scripture is a sharp blade, with the capacity to heal and repair just like a scalpel in a surgeon's hand. Unfortunately, it also can bruise and bludgeon like a butcher's knife. This book hopes to introduce some interpretive strategies that will promote the former and reject the latter.

As a social ethicist, my primary aim is to promote reading strategies that will help us to consider some of the pressing moral issues of our day. Thus, this is less a book on biblical studies and more a project in social ethics that tries to teach and appeal to responsible strategies of scriptural interpretation. Each section of the Bible we engage will move directly into reading with the explicit intent of addressing a particular pressing moral issue. Before his assassination, Martin Luther King Jr. identified poverty, racism, and militarism as interrelated triple evils of violence that perpetuate a vicious cycle of human suffering. When we couple this with King's persistent denunciation of materialism and constant call for a revolution of values from a "thing-oriented society to a person-oriented society," we begin to approximate how his much-talked about dream of a just society was far from an ephemeral vision. Like that of the Hebrew prophets, King's moral vision emerged from a thoroughgoing social analysis of the unjust structures and insidious cultural habits of the nation.

The interrelated injustices of poverty, racism, classism, and materialism of King's twentieth century have given way to an immoral host of plagues in our twenty-first century. Not surprisingly, the most pressing injustices of our day have the most harmful effects on the most vulnerable. Despite great social strides among all groups, an economic gap has left the poor and working class behind. Here I am thinking of the effects of gross income inequality, particularly on working women and members of the LGBTQ community, who are more susceptible to gender discrimination and sexually hostile work environments. The militarization of local police departments and the growth of the prison industrial complex have led to increased surveillance and disproportionate imprisonment in poor black and brown neighborhoods. Furthermore, we have been willing to place profit over people and political power over moral character.

Many want to know if there is a word from the Lord to speak to these unjust and destructive social arrangements. Yes, there is. We can address such suffering in our world only when we approach the Bible carefully yet imaginatively, and faithfully yet responsibly.

**For Further Reading**

Bird, Jennifer. *Permission Granted: Take the Bible into Your Own Hands.* Louisville, KY: Westminster John Knox Press, 2015.

Blount, Brian K., and Leonora Tubbs Tisdale. *Making Room at the Table: An Invitation to Multicultural Worship.* Louisville, KY: Westminster John Knox Press, 2000.

Goff, Philip, Arthur E. Farnsley II, and Peter Thuesen, eds. *The Bible in American Life.* New York: Oxford University Press, 2017.

Gushee, David P. *Still Christian: Following Jesus out of American Evangelicalism.* Louisville, KY: Westminster John Knox Press, 2017.

Warner, Laceye C. *Saving Women: Retrieving Evangelistic Theology and Practice.* Waco, TX: Baylor University Press, 2007.

# 2

## Taking the Bible Seriously

### The Ethics of Biblical Interpretation

> I do not feel obliged to believe that the same God who has
> endowed us with sense, reason, and intellect has intended
> us to forgo their use.
>
> —Galileo Galilei

> Sometimes the Bible in the hand of one man is worse
> than a whiskey bottle in the hand of [another]. . . . There
> are just some kind of men who—who're so busy worrying
> about the next world they've never learned to live in this
> one, and you can look down the street and see the results.
>
> —Miss Maudie, *To Kill a Mockingbird*

The term *biblical criticism* is enough to make
many people of faith uncomfortable. In common
parlance, the word *critical* has become synony-
mous with a negative and skeptical sentiment. Thus, any critical approach to Scripture is assumed to be faith averse. There
is also an exaggerated and unfortunate caricature of biblical
scholars that has gained purchase in our society. Too often, biblical studies professors are depicted as the high priests of skep-
ticism. From atop their perch in the ivory tower, they study the

Bible solely as a collection of literary texts and mythic tales, with the sole purpose of debunking and disproving that which people of faith hold dear.

These sorts of misrepresentations and misunderstandings about biblical scholarship have fostered suspicion toward, if not outright scorn for, scholars of religion. This is unfortunate. Such misconceptions have created a gulf between communities of faith and the academic enterprise. This is unnecessary. There is no need for us to lose sight of the ways these groups can and should inform one another.

The best preachers in America are powerful biblical scholars in their own right. Amy Butler of the Riverside Church in New York City and Eugene Cho, founding pastor of the Quest Church in Seattle, come quickly to mind. These are thoughtful, scholarly interpreters of the Bible who profess their Christian faith from pulpits every Sunday morning. Similarly, the Society of Biblical Literature (SBL), the professional scholarly guild of biblical studies, is full of academicians who view scholarship as their ministerial vocation, a confession of their Christian faith. Wilda C. Gafney and Francisco Lozada Jr. of Brite Divinity School and Nyasha Junior of Temple University are examples.

The intent of biblical criticism is not to disparage or denigrate, but rather to explain and illumine. As people of faith, we should remember that the opposite of faith is not doubt; it is certainty. We must resist the temptation to declare that we know for certain the meaning of Scripture. Biblical interpretation must remain an open and ongoing process.

Every translation that we have of the Bible is a result of the interpretive, or **hermeneutic**, process. The very act of translating the Hebrew Bible and New Testament from their original Hebrew and Greek is a form of interpretation. Whenever we open up a Bible, whether it is the King James Version, the New International Version, the New Revised Standard Version, or another translation, we are reading the results of scholarly interpretation. Moreover, consider the very compilation of the sixty-six books that we now refer to as the Bible, a term that derives from the Latin *biblia*, meaning "the books." The book that we think of as a unified sacred document is the result of a protracted and often contested process known as canonization. The Hebrew Bible took more than six hundred years to reach its current form, and the New Testament another three hundred years.

The books of the Hebrew Bible, more commonly known as the Old Testament, were compiled over several stages. The first five books are known as the **Pentateuch**, a combination of the Greek *penta* ("five") and *teukhos* ("scrolls"). Also referred to as the Law, the five scrolls of the Pentateuch were considered sacred by around 400 BCE. Before this, the classic stories of the first five books were traditional oral narratives told and transcribed in different ways by different peoples over centuries. Now you can see why the Bible is so confusing to read at times. The seemingly endless lists, repeated phrases, and similar storylines among different characters are the remnants of oral forms and imitations of earlier written documents.

The writings known as the Prophets began to take form as early as the eighth century BCE and continued to develop through the period of exile into the fourth century BCE. Along with the books of Isaiah, Jeremiah, and Hosea, the Prophets also include the books of Joshua, Judges, Samuel, and Kings. These writings were not compiled and accepted formally as part of the Old Testament until around 200 BCE. Much of the Prophets serves as a continuation of the history of God's promises to Abraham and the fulfillment of this covenant when Israel secures the land and establishes a monarchy. We refer to this as the Deuteronomistic History, since the book of Deuteronomy emphasizes God's covenant and faithfulness. This is why I will refer to the books of Samuel and Kings as Dynastic literature, as they offer an account of King David's rise along with his successors, a key point of emphasis in chapter 4.

The twenty-seven books of the New Testament were written after Jesus' death, roughly between 45 and 100 CE. It was another three hundred years before early church leaders could agree on what documents warranted designation as authoritative, sacred texts. As Paul Wegner explains so well in his book *The Journey from Texts to Translations: The Origin and Development of the Bible*, influential theologians such as Clement of Rome in the first century, Irenaeus in the second century, and Tertullian and Origen in the late second and third centuries were hardly uniform in their judgments. One example involves the authorship of the Letter to the Hebrews. Origen was willing to concede that Paul wrote Hebrews, even though he had his doubts. Since Paul was considered an apostle, church leaders automatically deemed his writings worthy of canonization. But Tertullian believed Hebrews to have been written by Barnabas, Paul's missionary accomplice, whose writings were not considered worthy.

Debates did not end there. Some Gospel texts associated with early Christian communities were excluded altogether, and there were ongoing disputes over books that eventually made the cut, such as the Letters of James and Jude. There were those who believed James contradicted the book of Romans and was thus not worthy of canonization. But since the book of James is attributed to James, the brother of Jesus, the final decision resulted in its inclusion.

Compiling and canonizing the texts of the Bible spanned over seven hundred years, and conflict about their meaning and relative importance has never ceased. Biblical texts have always been up for debate. There is not now, nor has there ever been, a singular way to view Scripture. As the late professor Daryl Schmidt was known for telling his entering biblical studies students at Texas Christian University, "You can take the Bible literally, or you can take it seriously."

### The Word of God in Human Hands

To take the Bible seriously is to understand it as a divinely inspired text, the word of God. Despite the pervasive use of this phrase in Protestant circles, there is little clarity and even less consensus concerning its meaning. Christians often cite 2 Timothy 3:16: "All scripture is inspired by God and is useful for teaching, for reproof, for correction, and for training in righteousness." But what does it mean for us to declare the Bible as divinely inspired?

Many Christians regard biblical writers as mere transcribers and ancient stenographers who recorded the divine dictates of God. All the historical and literary evidence that we have about the Bible's original composition and subsequent canonization refutes such a view. Ancient authors captured their experiences with the Divine according to the words, concepts, and categories known to them. From Genesis to Revelation, biblical writers describe God only symbolically and metaphorically. Well-known statements such as "The Lord is my shepherd" and "The Lord God is a sun and shield" are examples of biblical writers' sincere attempts to capture and convey a community's understanding of God. They wrote human descriptions of sacred realities.

Symbolic and metaphorical language, however, always needs a context to make sense. What may appear as an appropriate description of religious experience among one group can come across as foreign and confusing to another. Social context determines meaning. Let's consider a contemporary example. If someone attends a political rally in the United States and wears a T-shirt with an elephant on it, it is safe to conclude that they are supporting the Republican Party. Elsewhere, an elephant represents a Hindu deity or membership in a particular college sorority. For us to know the where and the when is thus essential to communication and comprehension. This was also true among biblical writers and their intended audiences. Scripture provides us with beautiful and poetic images that alluded to familiar, conventional images of the ancient world. The writers were informed and limited by their eras, social locations, and theological agendas. Authors referenced the symbols with which they were most comfortable within a worldview that they often took for granted.

For this reason, I need to make two interrelated claims about the Bible. On the one hand, I believe the Bible to be a collection of inspired writings and sacred narratives that point us toward God. On the other hand, I do not believe that divine inspiration supplanted or superseded the human faculties of biblical writers. God can inspire. Gospel writers, for instance, conveyed moral truths from Jesus that have resonated with people in several historical eras and across many different cultures. But God does not lift writers out of their historical and cultural context. Consider that legend states that God inscribed the Ten Commandments on two tablets of stone for Moses. Would it not have been easier to make the commandments appear on a tablet computer? Similarly, Moses struck a rock to bring forth water in the desert. Would not a water cooler or portable water bottles have been more convenient? My somewhat playful point here is simple. If God is infinite, biblical writers were limited; though God transcends time, the human beings who penned Scripture blossomed within these historical circumstances. Human involvement always dilutes the divine, just as human sinfulness negates any possibility of so-called biblical inerrancy.

Moreover, because we affirm the Bible as divinely inspired words ought not to mean that we need to regard ancient writings as final. This may seem blasphemous. However, consider that we live in a very different world than the biblical writers. Moral problems, scientific discoveries, and new insights into the human condition challenge us in ways that the apostle Paul would never have fathomed. Writers of scriptural texts could no more imagine our context, the challenges we face, and the information we now possess about the physical world than you and I can imagine life on planet Earth two thousand years from now.

Although some preachers and theologians proclaim that God never changes, people do. And our world does, too. In the words of New Testament professor, Presbyterian minister, and president of Union Presbyterian Seminary Brian K. Blount, at the 2000 Covenant Conference, "God, you remember Jesus saying, is a God of the living, not the dead. But a last word is necessarily a dead word. It stops listening. It stops learning. It stops living!" Therefore, if we are going to allow the teachings of the Bible to inform our lives and ethical choices, we must be open to God challenging us through biblical narratives in a way that speaks to someone living in North America in the twenty-first century, as opposed to first-century Palestine. We cannot allow the biblical writers, with their historical, cultural, and personal limitations, to have the last word on matters of violence against children, the subjugation of women, or the enslavement of one human being by another anymore than we can allow contemporary levels of acceptance of war, the inequality of women, and human trafficking to be the last word on these matters.

### Uncovering Clues in the Ancient World

Taking the Bible seriously also includes the process of **exegesis**. The term *exegesis* is derived from the Greek terms *ex* ("out of") and *hegeomai* ("to lead"), thus literally "to lead out of." Over time, the verb became associated with literary texts and leading out the proper meaning. Exegesis is thus used to describe the act of interpreting a passage of Scripture by appropriately identifying or leading out the meaning of the text based on factors such as knowledge of the original language, author, and intended audience. It demands that we piece together clues about the historical sources and contexts that informed the production of Scripture.

My use of the term *clues* here is intentional. One of my favorite professors in seminary likened the exegetical task to detective work. He would say that our job as biblical interpreters is to sleuth around the ancient world. I have encouraged Bible study participants to imagine themselves as lead detective on an imaginary show, *CSI: Ancient Israel*. Like the popular television franchise *Crime Scene Investigation*, biblical narratives are full of deception, crimes of passion, and tales of revenge, as well as stories of people of goodwill attempting to counter humanity at its worst with care and compassion. We can turn our nose toward discovery, uncover clues, and infer conclusions from evidence left at the scene.

Exegesis begins with four simple questions: Who? When? Where? What? The answers to these questions can reveal important details about the influences and circumstances around a book's production and particular communities of faith under consideration. If Moses did not write the first five books of the Bible, for instance, then who did? When did the Egyptians enslave the Hebrews? Where was the apostle Paul put to death? What were the charges that led to his presumed execution? Beyond these more historical questions, there is another dimension to exegesis: What did the term *faith* mean for biblical writers? What was Paul's relationship to slavery, and how did it inform his view of God's kingdom? Finding the answers to these questions involves the task of exegesis.

All texts possess various dimensions of meaning with no single way to answer these questions. It is possible to encounter different aspects of a text, have a partial understanding of it, and come to different conclusions than others. This is because there are multiple interpretive approaches that one might take. Here I will mention briefly three of the more traditional and broad exegetical methods in biblical studies: literary criticism, historical criticism, and theological criticism.

The literary approach examines the words of the scriptural text, their composition, and how they convey an intended message. Literary critics pay particular attention to the style of writing to determine the who, when, and where, and the primary purpose is often identified in the form or genre of writing. Historical criticism examines Scripture as a historical document representative of a particular period. This approach encourages us to ask questions about events and primary sites mentioned in the text, as well as the presence of the main historical figures that may shed light on the era. Historical criticism helps us to uncover the realities of people's lives during specific time periods. Finally, theological criticism examines Scripture primarily as an articulation of beliefs about God. Interpreters focus on sacred accounts concerning the origins and ultimate aims of creation, the nature of good and evil, and notions of sin, redemption, and God's ultimate plan of salvation. Theological critics raise questions about the attributes of God, the scriptural sources of particular doctrines, and what ways these attributes or doctrines should govern human activity and morality.

Each of these approaches to biblical exegesis has immense value for the interpretive task. But when used independently of the other methods, the literary, historical, or theological approach can blind us to other dimensions of the biblical text that are essential for reading the Bible in its world for our world. Thus, it is important for us as aspiring interpreters to understand that there are many different ways to figure out the who, when, where, and what. Similar to the ways that detectives consider multiple clues to approximate the how and why of a crime, the strongest biblical interpretations consider multiple perspectives in tandem. I have come to believe that we find the most compelling descriptions at the intersection of literary, historical, and theological approaches placed in conversation with the social context of biblical writers. More importantly, when we develop a better understanding of how ancient storytellers understood God in relation to their own social experiences in their historical moment, it will shed even more light on the meaning of the text. It is just a matter of us uncovering cultural scripts that biblical writers took for granted about themselves and their audience. Such cultural scripts are central to the sociohistorical approach to Scripture.

## Learning Cultural Scripts

Cultural scripts are key themes, prevailing attitudes, and social roles that inform how people relate to one another in a given context. This may include vocabulary as well as power relations that shape how stories are formed and received. For those who are familiar with the social world of a writer, the cultural script adds levels of complexity and detail that others may miss or, even worse, misinterpret.

Let me give a contemporary example. I am an avid sports fan and grew up playing football. In fact, my suburban Atlanta neighborhood, like many others in the southern United States, considered Friday night high school football as more than a sport; it was a religion. Football had its rituals for the community: the singing of "The Star-Spangled Banner," standard cheers, the syncopated beats of the drum line, and the communal head-nodding to the pep band's rendition of Cameo's "Talkin' Out the Side of Your Neck." There was also a shared language and an assumed pattern of behavior for the players— a cultural script. On the field, we would bang helmets, punch one another with great force, and call one another "baby" or "dawg" as ways of expressing excitement and encouragement. Invariably, these continue to be the sort of rituals we enact while watching football today. Professional, middle-aged, arthritic men assume the cultural scripts of adolescent athletes of decades ago.

The first time my children accompanied me to a professional football game, they felt that my friends and I were more entertaining than anything on the field. They peppered us with questions afterward: "Why did you guys hit and push each other like you were angry when your favorite team scored?" "Don't you think it's a little weird that you guys were hugging and screaming, 'Yeaaaaah, baby!'?" Beyond pointing out that yours truly acts like a moron at sporting events, there is another point to this story. Certain phrases and expressions between my childhood best friend and me need no explanation. To my twins, however, our behaviors appeared foreign and odd. The twins' response to and questions about my behavior reveal the interpretive gap between our worlds.

The same applies to stories that we read in the Bible. Biblical writers could take rhetorical shortcuts to represent what would have been otherwise familiar to their audience. The same is true for the way they portrayed power, cultural differences, and class distinctions. In the New Testament, for instance, Samaritans are often presented in contrast to Judeans. This is because most Judeans viewed Samaritans as their enemies. Biblical storytellers used Samaritans to teach lessons about overcoming cultural difference and redefining the boundaries of who Judeans might consider their neighbor. Thus, a thorough understanding of social context can help us understand meaning and even imagine the reception of early listeners to a biblical story.

The sociohistorical approach also provides a way to interrogate gender dynamics in the ancient world. The emergence and work of feminist theologians and biblical scholars has helped us to view the ancient world from the perspective of women. This includes garnering a better understanding of women's social environments and then moving the experiences of women in Scripture to the center of the narrative. The groundbreaking work of my Harvard colleague Elisabeth Schüssler Fiorenza offers a fine example. Her pioneering books point toward the sociohistorical approach and are primarily concerned with the historical, social, and rhetorical circumstances of women in Scripture. Biblical history becomes biblical "herstory" insofar as the religious experiences of women such as Phoebe and Chloe are not submerged under Paul but are recognized as significant in their own right. Schüssler Fiorenza's work identifies the egalitarian impulses that were central to Jesus's ministry and the way subsequent patriarchal biblical writers diminished Jesus' just treatment of women.

A new generation of scholars has expanded the sociohistorical approach beyond the examination of religious, economic, and gender hierarchies to consider the ways other categories of difference such as ethnicity contributed to early forms of cultural bias and prejudice. *Prejudice and Christian Beginnings: Investigating Race, Gender, and Ethnicity in Early Christian Studies* is a collection of essays edited by Schüssler Fiorenza and another one of our colleagues, Laura Nasrallah, about how human value and social worth were linked to particular social identities. Just as the categories of white, black, Christian, Jewish, Muslim, native born, immigrant, Asian American, Hispanic, Mexican, middle class, and working class are often freighted with assumptions about whether someone is a success or a failure, smart or stupid, hardworking or lazy, honest or criminal, insider or outsider, educated or uneducated, there were similar categories within the Roman Empire. It mattered whether one was a Roman, a Galilean, a Samaritan, or a widow. These markers of identity helped to determine one's social standing. A sociohistorical approach, then, contributes to our understanding of biblical writers' view of the world, as well as God's role in it.

## Unpacking Our Own Interpretive Baggage

Just as biblical writers brought their own social experiences and understandings of God to a text, you and I, as interpreters, do so as well. We do not come to the Bible as blank slates void of assumptions, expectations, and inclinations. Who we are impacts how we read. All of us assume different things about the Bible and God before engaging a text. Two truisms about biblical interpretation and devotion illustrate this point well. First, what we assume about God informs what we expect from God. If we understand God to be loving and kind, we will expect God's grace and compassion more than God's wrath and judgment. Second, what we assume about God will inform who we will become. Thus, if we worship a judgmental, impersonal, and stern God, it should be no surprise when we project a judgmental, aloof, and stern face of God to others. We are what we worship.

Alice Walker provides a poignant example of this in her classic novel *The Color Purple*. The book's primary character, Celie, spends her life under the dehumanizing physical blows of men. Writing letters to God seems to be her only outlet and means of maintaining relative sanity. At a certain point, however, this practice begins to fail her. A conversation with her friend Shug reveals that her assumptions about God are now leading to the disconnect. When asked about the image of God to which she has been praying, Celie replies, "The God I been praying and writing to is a man. And act just like all the other mens [sic] I know. Trifling, forgetful and lowdown." Shug helps Celie to realize that God transcends gender, race, and all of the other social constructs that humans attribute to God. Celie is then able to conceptualize a God that is much broader and more beautiful than she previously imagined. Celie begins to see God in nature, including the beauty of the color purple in the field. Her last letter addressed to God starts with the salutation, "Dear God. Dear stars, dear trees, dear sky, dear peoples. Dear everything. Dear God." We see from the perspective of Celie that our assumptions and expectations shape our reading of Scripture. Our own limitations and culture always and already affect how we think about and read Scripture. As interpreters, we need to pay attention to what we bring to the texts and what we read into texts. Such an honest assessment of our assumptions is a critical dimension to responsible biblical interpretation.

There is an interesting tale about the personal nature of scriptural interpretation. Several men went to the Buddha to settle a dispute between preachers and scholars who had wildly different views. The Buddha proceeded to share a parable about blind men describing an elephant. The man who felt the head described the elephant like a pot, the man who felt the tusk likened the elephant to a plow, and the man who felt the foot defined an elephant as a pillar. The Buddha concluded with a poem:

O how they cling and wrangle, some who claim ·
For preacher and monk the honored name!
For, quarreling, each to his view they cling.
Such folk see only one side of a thing.

This Buddhist parable captures the heresy of certainty that can derail responsible biblical interpretation among Christians. To recognize one's social location, theological commitments, and other biases as an interpreter is to humbly acknowledge that while one's reading of Scripture might be correct in part, it is always incomplete. We are often blinded by our own perspective and cling too tightly to our own limitations.

## Getting Started

I have presented a lot of information regarding biblical history, biblical criticism, and interpretation in this chapter. You may be thinking, "Where should I begin?" Let me try to distill several points from this chapter in order to put us on a path to responsible scriptural interpretation. Following prayer and meditation, biblical interpretation begins for me with three important steps. First, capture the big picture. This can help answer questions about the literary form, the author, and the intended audience. A good study Bible can prove a valuable resource in helping to respond to such questions and in establishing the boundaries of a particular text. For instance, reading a psalm is very different from reading one of Paul's letters. Psalms is a collection of liturgical poetry, whereas each Epistle is often complete and intended to be read in its entirety; the Epistles are occasional letters, not a letter packet from the apostle. Knowing what I am reading and how it should be read is a critical first step.

The second step involves consulting a solid secondary source. Reading literature about a text by a trained biblical scholar is necessary. This may take the form of an expository biblical commentary that will provide many details of the text and its context. I appreciate commentaries that locate the text in the original context in order to attend to the social background, introduce devotional elements for daily application, and pull from the broad range of biblical scholars. Another helpful resource are books that attend to particular sections of the Bible, such as the Pentateuch, Wisdom literature, the Gospels, or the writings of Paul. Fortunately, thanks to modern technology, there is no need to find the closest theological library. The works of leading biblical interpreters of the Hebrew Bible and New Testament are readily available online and through ebooks.

To be clear, all writings on the Bible are not equal. Anyone with a computer can publish a creative reading of Scripture. Make sure to consult articles or books from a reputable source. When I am looking for a book on a given topic, I know I can trust certain publishers that have put the author through a process of review by other established experts. If I do not recognize an author, then I can check the publisher. University presses are always a great place to start. There are also denominational and other religiously oriented publishing houses that specialize in high-quality biblical studies. Westminster John Knox Press and Fortress Press are important imprints. You can also trust IVP Academic (the academic imprint of InterVarsity Press) and HarperOne (an imprint of HarperCollins) to publish quality scholars of religion.

The third step is to own the biases that we each bring to Scripture. We can only pray for God's spirit to stretch us beyond the borders of our comfort zones once we acknowledge the reality of our social position. For instance, as a relatively privileged, heterosexual male in the developed world, it may be easier for me to gravitate toward interpretations that underscore God's favor on my life. God's support of Joshua's military might, David's royal power, or Solomon's wealth might readily resonate with me. But how about those characters in Scripture who are least like me—for example, women, the poor, and those living along the social margins? As we will see in the next chapter, there are times when we might identify with the great Hebrew patriarch Abraham. Yet there might be other times where God wants us to identify with those for whom Abraham's actions harm and endanger. When we acknowledge the perch from which we are most inclined to read a text, we are better prepared to put on God's lenses of love and see what God sees.

**For Further Reference**

Billing, J. Todd. *The Word of God for the People of God: An Entryway to Theological Interpretation of Scripture*. Grand Rapids: Wm. B. Eerdmans Publishing Co., 2010.

Brueggemann, Walter, William C. Placher, and Brian K. Blount. *Struggling with Scripture*. Louisville, KY: Westminster John Knox Press, 2002.

*Feasting on the Word: Preaching the Revised Common Lectionary*. Louisville, KY: Westminster John Knox Press, 2008–2011.

*Interpretation: A Bible Commentary for Teaching and Preaching*. Louisville, KY: Westminster John Knox Press, 1982–2005.

Junior, Nyasha. *An Introduction to Womanist Biblical Interpretation*. Louisville, KY: Westminster John Knox Press, 2015.

Lozada, Francisco, Jr. *Soundings in Cultural Criticism: Perspectives and Methods in Culture, Power, and Identity in the New Testament*. Minneapolis: Fortress Press, 2013.

Mack, Burton L. *Who Wrote the New Testament? The Making of the Christian Myth*. San Francisco: HarperOne, 1996.

*The New Interpreter's Bible: A Commentary in Twelve Volumes*. Nashville: Abingdon Press, 1998.

# 3

## Seeing as God Sees

### Putting on the Lenses of Love

> To love someone means to see him as God intended him.
> —Fyodor Dostoyevsky

> Wisdom is qualitatively different than smartness. And maturity is qualitatively different than braininess. I am not against smartness and braininess, but it just falls so radically short of wrestling with what it means to be human and making the right mature choices in life.
> —Cornel West

#### One Love

From Genesis to Revelation, there is a dominant theme throughout the Bible: God sides with those on the underside of power. Consider first the Hebrew Bible. From the story of slavery in Egypt to that of exile in Babylon, the most memorable narratives involve a God who stands over against systems of oppression. Similarly, the Hebrew prophets speak of God's care for the most vulnerable in Israel whenever the leaders "trample the head of the poor into the dust of the earth, and push the afflicted out of the way" (Amos 2:7).

The life and ministry of Jesus of Nazareth also capture this view of God. According to Luke, Jesus inaugurates his ministry by quoting from Isaiah: "The Spirit of the Lord is upon me, because he has anointed me to bring good news to the poor. He has sent me to proclaim release to the captives, and recovery of sight to the blind, to let the oppressed go free" (Luke 4:18). Couple this scene with what has to be considered Jesus' boldest and bravest parable—in Matthew 25, where he teaches about the day of judgment—and Jesus reveals to us a God who identifies most with those who are hungry, thirsty, strangers, ill, and imprisoned. For as we treat them, we treat God.

Entering a text trying to see what God might see and trying to land in a place where God's love seeks to abide are consistent with the overarching spirit of Scripture. Saying that I attempt to see what God might see is in no way a claim to have the mind, awareness, or comprehension of God. But I try to put on the lenses of love to look for those with whom God most aligns, the marginalized and victimized. I aim to step inside of a text and search for the lonely, the left out, and those who have been left behind. Here we will find the Spirit of God and God's radical love for us.

This is what it means for me to approach Scripture with a critical mind and sensitive heart. Intellect is never divorced from moral character. To show compassion requires that one demonstrate a critical understanding of social customs, laws, and structures of a given society. Knowing the stated (and unstated) rules that govern a society helps a reader better identify the people who are most likely to be privileged, as well as those who are most likely overlooked. Compassion coupled with a comprehensive understanding of society cultivate a moral disposition of love and care. Simply put, we need both our head and heart to show love.

In calling for such an intellectual disposition, I am challenging a way of moral reasoning that seeks to divorce the "rational" (read: brain) from the "affective" (read: feelings and emotions). Traditionally, notions of ethical decision-making informed by the Enlightenment called for dispassionate and objective analysis. Feelings, intuition, and emotion were supposed to be brought under the control of rational, logical reasoning. This is a fool's errand. We human beings are social creatures who are always and already informed by cultural patterns, past experiences, and sacred stories that shape how we see the world and process daily interactions. While scientific data, empirical verification, and deliberative, well-informed decisions are important, deeply embedded feelings, anxieties, and aspirations shape the choices human beings make as well. Emotions matter.

Here I find the Wisdom literature of the Hebrew Bible helpful. The purpose of wisdom literature in the ancient world was not very different than it is today. Elders in the community passed down inherited lessons on life and living to develop the personal character of young people and to explain inexplicable aspects of life. Wisdom here is not tied to smarts as much as to virtue. The Greeks called this *phronesis*, or practical wisdom linked to personal character. As an example, Proverbs 4:20–27 reads:

> My child, be attentive to my words;
>     incline your ear to my sayings.
> Do not let them escape from your sight;
>     keep them within your heart.
> For they are life to those who find them,
>     and healing to all their flesh.
> Keep your heart with all vigilance,
>     for from it flow the springs of life.
> Put away from you crooked speech,
>     and put devious talk far from you.
> Let your eyes look directly forward,
>     and your gaze be straight before you.
> Keep straight the path of your feet,
>     and all your ways will be sure.
> Do not swerve to the right or to the left;
>     turn your foot away from evil.

At the outset, the writer encourages readers to keep these teachings within their hearts for living a productive life. The writer is not sentimental or maudlin. To the contrary, the writer makes an intellectual argument, as the ancient Israelites did not make the division between the heart and the head. The Hebrew word for heart, *leb*, can also mean "mind" or "will." Israelites understood the heart as the center of knowledge. An encouragement to keep those teachings in the heart is acknowledging the heart as the center of moral decision-making.

This serves as the bedrock of Jesus' ethical teachings. For Jesus, demonstrating our love for God by seeking the good of others—an ethic known as agape love—sums up the law and the teachings of the Hebrew prophets. When religious leaders attempted to trip Jesus up in Matthew 22 by asking him what the greatest of all commandments was, Jesus replied, "'You shall love the Lord your God with all your heart, and with all your soul, and with all your mind.' Herein lies the greatest and first commandment. And a second is like it: 'You shall love your neighbor as yourself.'" The great educator and sociologist of religion Benjamin Elijah Mays summed up this concept brilliantly: "The love of God and the love of man are one love."

Among Mays's most notable students at Morehouse College was Martin Luther King Jr. King provided a beautiful example of this understanding of love in his final sermon, delivered on April 3, 1968. Addressing a packed audience in the Mason Temple Church of God in Christ headquarters in Memphis, Tennessee, less than twenty-four hours before his assassination, King expounded on one of the foundational aspects of agape love: seeking the good of others. King held neither a romantic nor a friendly conception of love but rather an understanding of love expressed in intentional acts of care and compassion, which is at the core of the Hebrew Bible and the heart of the gospel message. King looked to the parable of the Good Samaritan (Luke 10:25–37) in his iconic "I've Been to the Mountaintop" address.

Of course, the parable itself is about agape love, empathy, and identifying your neighbor in the unlikeliest of places. When a certain Jewish man fell among thieves along a dangerous highway, it was neither a Levite (a well-pedigreed Judean) nor a priest who stopped to provide assistance, but a Samaritan—a class of people who were considered religiously and culturally inferior to people of the faith in Judea and Galilee. Thus, Jesus subverts conventional wisdom and places empathy in the eyes of the one who would otherwise be considered a foreigner. Jesus wanted to make the point that the Samaritan could see as God sees. The Samaritan saw the victim through the lenses of love.

King took the parable one step further. Not only did he allow the hearer to witness the Samaritan's demonstration of agape love, but King went on to show concern for the presumed bad guys of the text. King described his own experience driving down this "winding, meandering road" during his first trip to Jerusalem. Because of this experience, King imagined the priest and Levite fearing for their own lives. King concluded, "So the first question that the Levite asked was, 'If I stop to help this man, what will happen to me?' But then the Good Samaritan came by. And he reversed the question: 'If I do not stop to help this man, what will happen to him?'"

King's retelling of this story models the ethical design of the parable. He demonstrates both an ethic of love and empathetic care without reducing one to the other. This is to say, we have the capacity and obligation to do what is right and to show concern for our neighbor whether we feel like it or not. When we strengthen our capacity to identify with others, and thus empathize with them, it is always easier to do right by them. Love and empathy, together, lead to justice. As my former teacher and now Harvard colleague Cornel West likes to say, "Justice is what love looks like in public."

## The Stories that Shape Us

Part of the genius of the "I've Been to the Mountaintop" address is in the way King blends multiple interpretive and ethical approaches. In locating himself and his readers within the story of the Good Samaritan, King employs an ethical approach philosophers refer to as **narrative ethics**, which focuses on the stories that shape us morally. The stories that frame our world have a normative dimension insofar as they inform how we ought to think, act, interact, and judge others. Narratives are at the core of our moral selves.

Duke University theologian Stanley Hauerwas's view of Scripture focuses on the power of sacred narrative that shapes the moral life. As Hauerwas writes in his classic primer on Christian ethics, *The Peaceable Kingdom*, "The Bible is fundamentally a story of a people's journey with their God. A 'biblical ethic' will necessarily be one that portrays life as growth and development." To be clear, I am more inclined to interpret and reinterpret Scripture than many virtue ethicists like Hauerwas. I am not as wedded to traditional interpretations of Scripture. Yet there is one area where we strongly agree. Knowing what one is "supposed" to do and actually making the right choices when the pressures of life encamp against us are two different things. Ethical decision-making is more affective and intuitive, thus revealing the importance of personal character born of communal narratives. Similar to how an athlete's practice regimen takes over when she is fatigued, our character serves as a sort of moral muscle memory when life becomes overwhelming.

This is why I appreciate Hauerwas's approach to Scripture. Narrative ethics beckons us into biblical stories as moral subjects. A reader is not a disengaged interpreter standing outside of a story. Rather, a narrative ethical approach asks us to insert ourselves into the text and to identify with the triumphs, trials, dilemmas, and disappointments of biblical characters. Moral principles are not deduced from a list of commandments in order to judge who is right and who is wrong. We immerse ourselves in the text, experience the hopes, fears, and concerns that define the narrative, and then locate the complete and complicated humanity of all moral actors in the story to develop moral sensibilities.

This approach to sacred narrative captures what it means to be a part of a healthy living tradition. Stories of the past are strong and noble enough to be uprooted from their original context without being destroyed, and thus they provide fresh meaning to the contemporary moment. Living traditions bring the insights of the past to a new age in ways that are both inspirational and decidedly relevant. Instead of being a static symbol or standard against which everything is measured, they are a productive component of one's fluid and ever expanding faith. These stories provide fresh meaning and insights applicable to our particular moment.

Is this not what a minister does each Sunday morning? Preachers seek to bring Jesus forward from the annals of antiquity in order that he may be pressed upon the hearts and minds of the contemporary hearer in real and relevant ways. One's illness today may not be an issue of blood, leprosy, or a withered hand. Yet knowing that one's life is special to God can bring added strength and comfort to the cancer patient going through chemotherapy or the young man recently diagnosed with HIV.

I witnessed this recently with a dear friend. She entered the summer the envy of many. She was smart and charismatic. She had a caring husband and two beautiful boys. A new tenure track job at a major research university even awaited her in the fall. Yet during the summer she was diagnosed with breast cancer. She spent the entire year in and out of hospital waiting rooms, undergoing multiple surgeries, and enduring debilitating chemotherapy. Though she entered the year an admitted "collapsed Catholic," having found the church's hierarchy, marginalization of women, and perceived abuses of power too much to stomach, she increasingly began to tap into the spiritual resources and sacred stories of her faith. She came to realize that though Catholic hierarchy and patriarchy was one aspect of her religious tradition, the Catholic Church of her childhood had granted her so much more. It provided powerful and productive stories.

My friend mined the resources of a healthy living tradition found in her faith. She recalled biblical stories of Jesus connecting with human beings even when they were at their lowest. Over time, no matter how her body felt or looked due to the rigors of chemotherapy, she told me that it was good for her to know that she was yet affirmed and loved by God. Likewise, God's command for us to love and care for one another resonated deeply with her during the year. Taking time to appreciate beauty, enjoy the quiet presence of loved ones, and seize moments of joy were all born of the sacred ritual practices of her contemplative Christian tradition. Just as the faithful have found delight and encouragement in the Psalms for millennia, this form of intentional spiritual mindfulness caused her to lift her mind from her illness and connect with those who the demands of life often cause us to take for granted. The narratives and experiences of ages past were shaped to comfort her in the present.

Narratives pass down the powers of tradition. The strengths of shared stories include shaping appropriate moral dispositions to confront contemporary challenges. Ancient biblical writers understood this point well. As the Baptist preachers of my youth were known to say, "One should never let the facts get in the way of a good story." Facts may inform, but stories shape our character. This is why biblical writers were so comfortable shaping history with stories. Stories can convey eternal truths that the facts of life often miss.

## When the Sun Moves

On more than one occasion I have distinguished between fact and truth. This is intentional. Although academic approaches to the Bible have aided us in identifying authorship, pinning down historical dates, and learning more about the ancient world, there is an underside to evidence-based knowledge. Our modern obsession with factuality and empirical verification can negatively impact the way we read and receive the Bible. Too many have made the interrelated mistakes of biblical literalism and crass reductionism.

Biblical literalists feel that they must defend the factuality of the Bible to the extent that they are willing to compromise scientific credibility. In the face of overwhelming evidence, scientific discoveries, and increased ways of knowing, a literal reading of the Bible will tempt the Christian community to excommunicate scientists and observers who provide powerful insights about the makeup of humanity and origins of society. Such biblical literalism leads to a crass reductionism insofar as its adherents think that they can only hear and receive the writings of the Bible through this modernist frame—that is, if they cannot historically verify that Jonah remained alive in the belly of the fish for three days and three nights, then the story cannot reveal any truths about God's love and capacity to forgive. As a result, too many confine their intellectual capacity with the spiritual straightjackets of fundamentalism. Conversations are shut down by literalism, and spiritual insights that might be otherwise gained from the Bible are foreclosed by the need to verify empirically every single detail.

One does not need to live long to realize that there are multiple forms of truth. There is the aesthetic truth: beauty. I cannot verify empirically or explain scientifically why the sound of Donny Hathaway singing "Come Ye Disconsolate" or Luther Vandross's rendition of Burt Bacharach's "A House Is Not a Home" transports me to a place of peace, joy, and tranquility no matter how many times I hear them. But I know it is true. Similarly, I would never question a couple who walks down the aisle in holy matrimony convinced that they are holding the hand of the most beautiful person they have ever met. I believe in the idiom "Beauty is in the eye of the beholder."

There are metaphorical and moral truths. Nobody I know

believes in talking lions or magical worlds behind closet doors. This has not prevented millions throughout the Western world from passing down C. S. Lewis's *The Lion, the Witch, and the Wardrobe* to subsequent generations on the basis of the manifold moral truths it conveys. Nor would many give any credence to tales of yellow brick roads, dancing scarecrows, and cowardly lions. But L. Frank Baum's book *The Wonderful Wizard of Oz* has encouraged many of us to look deep inside of ourselves for the things we desire on the path toward success. Simply put, stories can serve as metaphors that convey moral truths without being literally or factually verified.

Few express this philosophical and historical nuance better than novelist Toni Morrison. In one short but influential essay, "The Site of Memory," Morrison explains that the crucial distinction in her writings is not between fact and fiction, but rather fact and truth. She notes how literature is considered fiction when it is deemed a product of the imagination but falls into biography or nonfiction when traced to a publicly verifiable event. In the absence of detailed, personal accounts of historical subjects, a writer has nothing more than her imagination to reconstruct the interior life of historical subjects. The point Morrison makes here is that truth is usually concealed. Like the ancient goddess Veritas who Romans believed liked to hide in the bottom of wells, we can only find truth after considerable searching and expense. For Morrison, imagination contributes to the interpretive process that helps us to pull truth from out of her hiding place.

Think about the subjects Morrison most often writes about: African American women living on the underside in conditions of slavery, segregation, and sexism. The absence, if not intentional erasure, of personal accounts of the deepest longings and spiritual strivings of enslaved women in America necessitates what Morrison refers to as "literary archaeology." A writer is forced to investigate remaining historical sources and use her imagination to reconstruct an interior world of individuals whose sentiments have evaporated into the gases of history.

As an example, Morrison based her novel *Beloved* on the true story of an enslaved woman named Margaret Garner. Garner was fleeing slavery in Kentucky when U.S. marshals cornered her in Ohio. Garner opted to commit filicide by taking the life of her child rather than having her daughter grow up as an enslaved sexual toy forced to bear the children of her owner. Morrison's novel excavates the interior life of enslaved women by revealing their truth of sexual violence, despair, and alienation from their offspring. Though we cannot verify all the facts of Morrison's account, she sought to present the truth of slavery's horror and inhumanity.

Similarly, just because one might be able to challenge the facts of a biblical narrative does not necessarily mean that one disrupts the truth that it reveals. Just ask John Jasper, one of this nation's most popular preachers in the nineteenth century. Born in 1812, Jasper began preaching in Richmond, Virginia, while enslaved on a local tobacco plantation. Following the Civil War and his subsequent emancipation, Jasper organized the Sixth Mount Zion Baptist Church and became a favorite preacher among both black and white Baptists alike. He was best known for his sermon "The Sun Do Move," which he reportedly delivered over 250 times, including once before the Virginia General Assembly. Jasper based the sermon on Joshua 10:13: "And the sun stood still, and the moon stopped, until the nation took vengeance on their enemies. Is this not written in the Book of Jashar? The sun stopped in mid-heaven, and did not hurry to set for about a whole day."

Jasper used this sermon as evidence that God could move the sun across the sky. According to Jasper,

> Joshua showed in the sight of all Israel that the Sun Do Move, because he stopped it, by God's command, for a whole day, as the text states. If he stopped it, that proves that the sun was moving, and moving over Joshua and the Amorites, and of course they was nowhere else than on this here earth, and

consequently it was moving around the earth, and after the battle was over, it begun moving again in its regular course.

Many in the community scoffed at what they regarded as Jasper's intellectual and religious primitivism. Some whites and formally educated African Americans saw him as the quintessential ignorant preacher. But for Jasper, if God said he stopped the sun, God apparently moved it. We can verify empirically that the earth revolves around the sun and not vice versa. This fact is undeniable. Nevertheless, what might it mean for us to understand Jasper's emphasis as not necessarily on the fact of the sun moving, but rather on the truth of God's power from the perspective of the formerly enslaved?

Jasper was forty years old when the Civil War began, and like many of his hearers, he was taught to believe that servitude was a fact of life. Many white preachers even taught on the plantation that slavery was God's will. All evidence seemed to substantiate this claim as fact. An enslaved person like Jasper, who had no reason to trust in the facts of life, was forced to hold on to the moral truth that God intended for all people to be free. This sermon, then, may very well be interpreted as a matter of simple philosophical deduction: the facts of Southern society pointed to a lifetime of servitude. Others said the sun never moves. God had the power to liberate the enslaved. Thus, God has the power to move the sun to make it stand still! What we have, then, is a metaphorical claim ("the sun do move") to corroborate an abiding moral truth. No matter how dark the circumstances, God has the power to deliver.

The above examples reveal how we can imagine a world of love and justice. More specifically, this is the role of **moral imagination**, an orientation that emboldens us to transcend particularities of the present and imagine a radically different future. Think about what the protagonists of Richard Bach's classic tale *Jonathan Livingston Seagull* and Robert Frost's poem "The Road Not Taken" share in common. They were both able to envision a different path forward that radically altered not only their individual lives but the lives of others. Many have employed the term *moral imagination*. From Edmund Burke in the nineteenth century, through John Dewey and T. S. Eliot, to more recent peace activists such as John Paul Lederach, moral imagination often describes an awakened and creative consciousness, a consciousness that can create something out of nothing. Like a painter before a blank canvas or a sculptor with a block of stone, moral imagination turns us into ethical artists. Though economic and political factors may seem predetermined and limiting regarding our ability to act, moral imagination allows us to conceptualize opportunities beyond the apparent limits placed before us.

Moral imagination is similar to faith. Moral imagination challenges us to look at what appears to be nothing to identify something. It asks us to look upon those who are deemed nobody by society to see somebody loved by God! Like faith, moral imagination is both a noun and a verb. The writer of Hebrews said it well: "Now faith is the assurance of things hoped for, the conviction of things not seen" (Heb. 11:1). Faith is an assurance of the hope that we possess and a description of our actions. Moral imagination is something that we have, and it is something that we can enact.

Exercising our moral imagination should never be divorced from a thorough understanding of our social worlds as prescribed above. There's a truism: vision without execution is hallucination. We can say the same about people of faith who have spiritual imaginations without social understanding. As my grandmother likes to say, "There is no need in being heavenly minded if you are no earthly good."

Furthermore, moral imagination is central to an ethic of love and justice. When we immerse ourselves in a biblical narrative, moral imagination helps us identify with biblical characters; over time, this can improve our ability to empathize with others. In the same way that biblical narratives help us to reimagine what was possible in the ancient world, this same moral imagination can help us reimagine what is possible in our world regarding love and justice.

## Seeing Our Sisters in the Wilderness

Throughout this chapter, I have attempted to make the case that multiple impulses shape our ethical orientation and stories shape our character. Our lack of feeling and emotions toward others is what often causes us to miss their hopes, fears, and sorrows. If we strengthen our capacity to see and identify with the most vulnerable in the biblical text, it strengthens our capacity to see and identify with those who are most vulnerable in our world today.

I concluded the previous chapter with a reference to the patriarch Abraham in the book of Genesis. He is a prominent character in the Hebrew Bible whom biblical writers employed to teach long and lasting moral lessons about faith. Let's consider the birth story of Abraham's first son found in Genesis 16. It is an account of Abraham's first son, Ishmael, who was born not to Abraham's wife, Sarah, but to Sarah's young enslaved Egyptian handmaiden, Hagar.

Recall our steps for biblical interpretation: First, capture the big picture. We know this is a narrative about Abraham. When I look at Genesis 16, it is clear to me that I should not read this chapter in isolation. Both the previous and the following chapters provide pertinent details about Abraham's life and call. Second, we ought to consult a quality secondary source to better understand the sociohistorical context and cultural script of the storyteller. Knowing these details will assist us in placing ourselves within the text with lenses of love in order to look for the most vulnerable characters in the narrative. Finally, we should think about what we are bringing to the text as readers. Remember that this can impact our level of sensitivity to characters in the text. Think about the places God might want to stretch us beyond our comfort zones to inspire empathy for others.

Among biblical scholars and theologians who come closest to an empathetic, sociohistorical reading strategy is Delores J. Williams, the Paul Tillich Professor Emerita of Theology and Culture at Union Theological Seminary in New York. Williams is an early and leading voice of **womanist theology**, a theological orientation that pays particular attention to the experiences of women of African descent in particular and all women minoritized by any combination of racism, sexism, and classism in general. Her contemporary classic text *Sisters in the Wilderness: The Challenge of Womanist God-Talk* identifies the social structures of power over women and calls for a reimagining of gender and race relations in our world.

The book offers a reading of Genesis 16 that offers insight into the prevailing cultural script of the moment. There are several laws and customs operating in this narrative. We see that Sarah appears barren, a condition that significantly diminished the social status of even wealthy women in Israelite culture. Law and custom, however, provided Sarah with options for childbirth. Wealthy free women could bring their handmaidens to their husbands to serve as surrogates. Any child born to a wife's handmaiden was then deemed the wife's child. So Sarah goes to Abraham and declares, "You see that the Lord has prevented me from bearing children; go in to my slave-girl; it may be that I shall obtain children by her" (16:2). Abraham accepts Hagar, and Hagar conceives a child. Sarah is still Abraham's wife, and Hagar remains enslaved. This imbalance and abuse of power creates a conflict between Sarah and Hagar, a conflict undoubtedly fueled by jealousy, contempt, and insecurity.

When Sarah complains to Abraham, Abraham gives Hagar back to Sarah and takes a passive stance. He says to her, "Your slave-girl is in your power; do to her as you please" (v. 6) Sarah deals with Hagar harshly, causing Hagar to run into the wilderness. Only when God appears to Hagar and encourages her to return to the household does she go back to Abraham and bear him a son, Ishmael—who is ultimately pushed to the side in favor of Isaac, born of Sarah.

What do you see in this story? Traditionally, biblical commentaries center on Abraham and Sarah's relationship. They criticize Sarah's willingness to take God's promises of producing a great nation into her own hands. Her plan for Abraham to impregnate Hagar serves as an indictment of her lack of faith. Others locate this narrative in the long line of God favoring the younger brother over the older. Think about Abel over Cain, Isaac over Ishmael, and Jacob over Esau. The problem with both of these interpretations, however, is that they virtually ignore the most vulnerable character in the text, the enslaved handmaiden Hagar. She is just a prop on Abraham and Sarah's stage.

Delores Williams places Hagar at the center of the narrative. As an enslaved woman, Hagar is on the underside of the underside of gender oppression in this story. Though Sarah is victimized by patriarchal bias and abuse, as a wealthy, free woman, she still has options available to her that the enslaved Hagar does not. The body and reproductive capacity of enslaved women, according to the laws and customs of ancient Israel, belonged to slaveholders. Sarah chooses to align her relative power with Abraham's male privilege to force Hagar into surrogacy, which is little more than a euphemism for rape.

Williams connects this text to the lived experiences of African American women under the institution of slavery. Too many enslaved women in the Americas found themselves living under the specter of sexual violence at the hands of slaveholders while also having to protect themselves and their offspring from harsh retribution from the wives of slaveholders.

One need not look any further than Thomas Jefferson and his relationship with Sally Hemings. Hemings was the daughter of planter John Wayles and a woman he owned named Betty Hemings. When Wayles died, his daughter by his wife (and thus Sally's half-sister) inherited Hemings and her enslaved siblings. This daughter, Martha Wayles, was married to Thomas Jefferson, then a young planter and aspiring politician. Sally was a small child at the time. Following Martha's death, and, it is said, due to her close resemblance to her older half-sister, Thomas Jefferson took the enslaved Sally into his bedroom. Sally would go on to give birth to six children by the president of the United States and the founder of the University of Virginia. He was both father and owner of these children.

There are many examples of enslaved women living in non-consensual, or at least intimidating, sexual relationships and surrogate roles that are not recorded in American history but were just as brutal and nefarious. Unfortunately, such practices of male abuse of vulnerable women continued long beyond the Emancipation Proclamation. In 1935, at the height of the Great Depression, Ella Baker and Marvel Cooke published an article in the NAACP journal *The Crisis* titled "The Bronx Slave Market." They described the daily labor pool on 167th Street where women, not unlike Hagar, with few means and fewer resources, offered themselves to the service of the wealthy Sarahs and Abrahams of New York City. Baker and Cooke wrote this chilling description:

> Rain or shine, cold or hot, you will find them there—Negro women, old and young—sometimes bedraggled, sometimes neatly dressed—but with the in-variable paper bundle, waiting expectantly for Bronx housewives to buy their strength and energy for an hour, two hours, or even for a day at the munificent rate of fifteen, twenty, twenty-five, or, if luck be with them, thirty cents an hour. If not the wives themselves, maybe their husbands, their sons, or their brothers, under the subterfuge of work, offer worldly-wise girls higher bids for their time.

Unfortunately, this pattern continues. We can read the stories of Hagar and Sally Hemings in their worlds and connect them to gender imbalance and sexual abuse in our world. There have been several high-profile revelations in recent years of political leaders, business executives, and celebrities using their power as a weapon of sexual assault. Most of these occurrences, however, take place behind closed doors and out of sight. Despite the increasing number of courageous women who have come forward thanks to the #MeToo movement and other rallying cries denouncing sexual harassment, many more women remain hidden in the shadows as a result of gender power imbalance. Interestingly and poignantly, when God shows up to Hagar in the wilderness, she refers to God as "El Roi," the God who sees.

The empathetic theological insight and moral imagination of Delores Williams is instructive. She turns our attention to Hagar in the biblical world so that we might, like God, see not only Hagar but the conditions in our world that render her invisible. Williams's interpretation allows the reader to see the struggle and stresses of working-class women of all races in our society today who continue to bear the brunt of childcare and domestic responsibilities while being grossly underpaid. An imbalance of power makes women more susceptible to exploitation and abuse.

Today it has become popular to encourage women to sit down and then "lean in" in the boardroom to be seen and heard. Sarah indeed leans in to make her voice and her views known to Abraham. Does Hagar have this option? Is it enough to capitulate to the established patterns of power whether they be patriarchy, unbridled corporate capitalism, or limited access to higher education? Is it sufficient to encourage Sarah to lean in without questioning the hard line of division between those who are sitting at the table with Abraham and those women who clean up after the meeting? Try to hear the voice of Hagar. She is crying out from her world into our world for our attention. God sees. Do we?

**For Further Reading**

Hauerwas, Stanley. *The Peaceable Kingdom: A Primer in Christian Ethics.* Notre Dame, IN: University of Notre Dame Press, 1991.

Schüssler, Elisabeth Fiorenza. *In Memory of Her: A Feminist Theological Reconstruction of Christian Origins.* 10th anniversary ed. New York: Crossroad, 1994.

King, Martin Luther, Jr. *A Testament of Hope: The Essential Writings and Speeches.* Special anniversary ed. San Francisco: HarperOne, 2003.

Lederach, John Paul. *Moral Imagination: The Art and Soul of Building Peace.* New York: Oxford University Press, 2010.

Mays, Benjamin Elijah. *Seeking to Be Christian in Race Relations.* New York: Friendship Press, 1957.

Nasrallah, Laura, and Elisabeth Schüssler Fiorenza, eds. *Prejudice and Christian Beginnings: Investigating Race, Gender, and Ethnicity in Early Christianity.* Minneapolis: Fortress Press, 2009.

Nussbaum, Martha C. *Poetic Justice: The Literary Imagination and Public Life.* Boston: Beacon Press, 1997.

Smith, Mitzi J., ed. *I Found God in Me: A Womanist Biblical Hermeneutics Reader.* Eugene, OR: Cascade Books, 2015.

Williams, Delores. *Sisters in the Wilderness: The Challenge of Womanist God-Talk.* 20th anniversary ed. Maryknoll, NY: Orbis Books, 2013.

# PART II

## The Power of Sacred History

# 4

## Explaining the Inexplicable

### Sacred History and Suffering in the Dynastic Literature

God made man because he loves stories.

—Elie Wiesel

The doctrine of blind obedience and unqualified submission to any human power, whether civil or ecclesiastical, is the doctrine of despotism, and ought to have no place among Republicans and Christians.

—Angelina Grimke

#### The Power of Sacred History

The Dynastic literature provides an account of the rise and fall of Israel's monarchy. We begin here, seemingly in the middle of the Hebrew Bible, because many of the figures and events of this period can be historically verified independently of Scripture.[1] Historians and archaeologists have discovered facts about the Egyptian, Assyrian, Babylonian, and Persian

---

1. In 1993, archaeologists found a stone in northern Israel now known as the Tel Dan Stele that dates back to the ninth century BCE. A stele is a monument, typically made of stone, with an inscription—in this case, an inscription that references conflict with the kings of Israel, including "the house of David."

Empires that help us understand better biblical stories about Israel's monarchy and captivity. The Dynastic literature also provides the backdrop for the entire Hebrew Bible. The more familiar we are with this particular section of Scripture, the better we are prepared to engage broader parts of the Bible.

Many early and modern scholars agree that a national history for Israel began to take form when the nation was conquered by the Babylonians and subsequently exiled around 587 BCE. Though oral traditions and creation stories were always in circulation, the anxiety associated with mass displacement and isolation necessitated a coherent narrative of Israel's prehistory, rise, and fall as a nation. The psalmist asked, "How could we sing the Lord's song in a foreign land?" (137:4) To sing the Lord's song, there needed to be a shared story. It is the context in which most of the texts of the Hebrew Bible were recorded, as ancient Israel reconstructed its past and imagined its future. Thus, over time the sacred history of the Hebrew Bible developed to help the nation cope with mass displacement.

By **sacred history**, I am referring to a genre of storytelling and writing. The ancients had a different conception of history than we do today. Building on a host of oral narratives, the ancients turned popular tales and actual recorded events into venerated histories. These sacred historical accounts were both fact and fancy, animated by both evidence and aspiration. This is why we should not approach the Hebrew Bible as a nonfiction historical text akin to those used in a university classroom. In history books, serpents do not speak, seas do not miraculously split down the middle, and men do not survive inside of the bellies of large fish. As a genre, the sacred history found in the Hebrew Bible shares more in common with folkloric legends and myths that were common in the ancient world.

Many of you reading this book may feel uncomfortable with the use of the term *myth* to describe the stories of the Bible. My Bible study participants did not like it at all. When I introduced the topic, they hit me with a fair share of side-eyed glances, pursed lips, and "Hold up a second, Professor!" Fair enough. In our society, a myth has come to connote that which is not true. Images of the magical world of Disney, J. K. Rowling's Harry Potter series, and other such wildly imaginative creations come to mind. Though a four-letter word, *myth* does not have to be foul or disrespectful.

Myths that serve as the grist of sacred histories are not the property of the emotionally immature, intellectually lazy, or politically gullible. Sociologists and anthropologists have argued convincingly that myths play important functions in societies. Myths unify communities around common themes, sublime principles, and presumed noble ideals. They can underscore the best a society has to offer by identifying historical high moments in a nation's or group's history, emphasizing the attributes and accomplishments of heroic personalities, and rearticulating values associated with past success.

This idea of sacred history shouldn't be strange to us. American history is replete with mythic narratives based on the heroic deeds of exceptional historical actors. From honest Abe Lincoln to Ronald Reagan, tales of their courage, valor, and accomplishments are staples of American exceptionalism. We often embellish their lives and ascribe to them the character traits we admire to justify our current status and sanctify our aspirations. In fact, every presidential election cycle, we hear countless personal biographies that include testimonies of how hard work, perseverance, and faith allowed parents and ancestors, if not themselves, to overcome and achieve prosperity in a manner believed only possible in America.

Let me see if I can make this clear by providing a personal example. My father grew up in segregated North Carolina, was orphaned by the age of twelve, left college to join the Air Force, possessed an eighteen-inch neck, and was often mistaken in public for the 1980s professional wrestler known as the Junk Yard Dog. Did I mention that my father's name was John Henry Walton? Yes, he was the namesake of John Henry, the African American, steel-driving, workingman's folk hero who defeated a steam-powered hammer in a race through a mountain. Needless to say, lectures in my house on the themes of responsibility, hard work, and sacrifice were long and lasting. Whenever I complained about school or a teacher, my father would recount how he had to walk past the local school to attend the "colored" school in Raleigh. He talked about the stress and pressures associated with being the first African American in several different roles in the military and the Federal Aviation Administration. I knew these facts to be correct.

I found it odd, however, that it seemingly snowed twelve months a year in North Carolina when he was a child. Nor did I quite understand how he walked to and from school uphill in each direction, lived off a diet of bread and water, and could only afford to wear "rags" and hand-me-down clothing, though I saw plenty of pictures of him dapperly dressed in high school. As an adult, I now understand that over time my father's history—a history of which he deserves to be quite proud—took on a life of its own, full of embellished, rags-to-riches adornments. Actual events became narratives of inspiration and models of success. Though one might dispute some of my father's facts, the inspiring truth of his struggles was indisputable. This is the power of sacred history.

It was similarly true in ancient Israel. You may recognize the tale of a courageous young soldier who entered a one-on-one duel against a giant war hero from the enemy's camp. The undersized warrior struck down his giant opponent with one precise shot to the head. The popular David and Goliath legend probably comes to mind. In fact, this legend emerged from Egypt and is recorded in the *Story of Sinuhe*. It dates to around 1800 BCE, making it older than the oldest known biblical writing, and many deem it as one of the finest literary works of ancient Egypt. We can assume that those who desired to describe the courage of King David were familiar with this tale. Invariably, the *Story of Sinuhe* became part of Israel's sacred history to extol the heroic valor of their beloved king. It appears that storytellers in ancient Israel knew a cardinal rule of my fellow Baptist preachers: never let the facts get in the way of a good story!

## Making Sense of Suffering

It should be clear now that sacred histories are more often told to underscore the moral values and ethical commitments of a community than to provide factual accounts of historical events. We appeal to sacred history as a source of inspiration about the present and future, particularly in the face of inexplicable evil, injustice, and suffering. And while some may understandably critique this as an illusory religious opiate that ignores suffering, I do not want to go there too quickly. It is important to consider the ways in which sacred histories can play a vital role in helping people endure, face down, and even fight against extreme suffering.

We have already noted that the development of a sacred history for the Jewish people coincided with the era of Babylonian captivity. The period between 605 and 539 BCE was a particularly violent and devastating time, as King Nebuchadnezzar of Babylon besieged and destroyed the southern kingdom of Judah. In Ezekiel 5, the prophet provides a dramatic display of devastation. After shaving his head and beard—an act of public humiliation and disgrace—the prophet divides the fallen hair into three parts. He burns a third of his hair to represent those who will die from famine and disease. He strikes another third with a sword to signify those struck down by the Babylonian army. Then he tosses the final third of his hair into the wind as an example of those who will endure exile and dispersal from the land.

According to Israel's sacred history, the political seeds of this destruction were sown centuries earlier. First Kings 11 provides an account of Israel's split following the death of King Solomon around 925 BCE. One of Solomon's former military leaders, Jeroboam, led a revolt against Rehoboam, Solomon's son and successor to the throne. Jeroboam organized the ten northern tribes to reject Rehoboam's leadership, elect himself king, and establish the northern kingdom of Israel. Rehoboam maintained control over the southern tribes of Benjamin and Judah, which remained faithful to the house of David. For the next couple of centuries, the northern kingdom would become known as Israel and the southern kingdom Judah.

This civil war left both sides vulnerable. Egypt wasted little time in making its move to seize Jerusalem (1 Kgs. 14:25; 2 Chr. 12:1–12). King Shishak, most commonly identified as Pharaoh Shoshenq I, took control of the riches of Solomon's throne and made Judah into a vassal state of Egypt. This drained Judah's economic and military strength. The northern kingdom of Israel remained intact until the Assyrian Empire seized control in 722 BCE. Due to power struggles and tension between the Assyrian, Egyptian, and Babylonian Empires, Judah remained insecure and exposed for the next one hundred and fifty years as a colony. Thus, when Babylon won the war of the ancient Near East, Judeans went from being a semi-independent people to Babylon's prize of war.

Within this context of violence and despair, it makes sense that a displaced people would need a shared history. Israel having a stabilizing and coherent narrative about the past could help offset the instability of exile and mass displacement in the present. Moreover, there is the genuine theological question associated with this period: Why, Lord? The people needed a storyline to help them make sense of the seemingly nonsensical and carve out a semblance of hope in a situation that seemed hopeless. One might argue that the sacred history of the nation presented in Samuel, Kings, and Chronicles also provides a theological account to explain suffering.

Any theological account to explain the problem of suffering is known as **theodicy**. *Theodicy* comes from a Greek term that combines the words for God and justice. It aims to make sense of or justify God's goodness in light of contradictory evidence. Theodicy calls us to consider our sense of justice when human suffering impugns and indicts the sublime attributes we ascribe to God. Scottish philosopher David Hume articulated the questions at the core of theodicy most explicitly in his *Dialogues concerning Natural Religion*: "Is God willing to prevent evil, but unable? Then God is impotent. Is God able, but not willing? Then God is malevolent. Is God both able and willing? Then from where does evil come?"

These were the questions for Judeans suffering under the heavy weight of Babylon. They wanted to make sense of their situation. Therefore, the narrative provided in Samuel–Kings, as well as the sixth-century prophetic writings such as Jeremiah, Habakkuk, and Ezekiel, reads like an explanatory account of their condition. In describing the rise and fall of the nation, the writers appear to be answering the questions "How did this happen to us? Why did a good and just God allow us to be taken away into captivity?"

The sacred history of ancient Israel recorded in Samuel–Kings could rival any reality television show. Israel's national history is presented as a moral roller-coaster ride, with high moments soon followed by instances of greed and corruption. King David's story provides a clear example. He is greatly revered in the Hebrew Bible, which describes him as a "man after God's own heart" (1 Sam. 13:14). From courageously protecting his father's sheep to instilling courage and hope in his troops, David comes across as a moral exemplar of strong military leadership. Nevertheless, he has his share of moral failings along the way, which culminate in the decline of his throne. Most notably, David begins an affair with Bathsheba, the wife of one of his soldiers, Uriah. After sending Uriah to the front lines as an act of murder, David marries Bathsheba. The prophet Nathan condemns him (2 Sam. 11–12), and this judgment unleashes a wave of torrid events on David's children, including rape, incest, and murder.

First Kings places David's son Solomon within a similar narrative of meteoric rise and precipitous fall. Solomon's fame and subsequent reputation emerge from his wisdom and wealth. When given a blank check by God to request whatever he desires, Solomon does not ask for a long life, fortune, or fame. Realizing the limitations of his cognitive capacity and deficiencies of discernment, Solomon asks God for wisdom (1 Kgs. 3:3–14). God thus grants Solomon wisdom as well as all of the wealth he could ever desire.

In addition to Solomon's wisdom and wealth, however, the narrator of Kings identifies Solomon's principal moral weakness: hundreds of foreign wives. And like most tales of male indulgence, the mix of money, materialism, and misogyny become a debilitating intoxicant for the king. The people's respect for Solomon erodes, as he levies extreme taxes to subsidize his lavish building projects. His demonstrated favoritism for the capital city of Jerusalem and the southern tribe of Judah, which contains Jerusalem, alienates tribes to the north. And by erecting temples to foreign gods so that his wives might have a place to worship, Solomon loses the goodwill of many priests.

According to these narratives, God is not pleased with Israel's leaders. Their behaviors set into motion a downward spiral of corruption and deceit that divides and ultimately destroys the nation. The overall aim of the writers of Samuel–Kings is to illustrate that the moral choices of Israel's leaders caused God to remove God's protective and loving hand. Why are Judeans forced to sing the Lord's song in a strange land? Because the nation—in particular, its leaders—did not keep God's covenant and statutes.

The sacred history of the Dynastic literature should not be reduced to stories of gloom and doom. Merited suffering, linked to the possibility of ultimate hope for those who remain faithful to God, is the subtext of the Samuel–Kings narrative. Despite David's sins and merited punishment, God will keep God's promises to the people. Overall, David's virtues still outweigh his vices. David's name in Hebrew means "beloved," and the writer continues to describe him as a man after God's own heart. With all their gifts and failings, God promises both David and Solomon that their family will reign over Israel forever (1 Kgs. 9:5). This was good news for an exiled people. An embattled and exiled people could take comfort in knowing that trouble wouldn't last always. This was their story. This was their song.

## Who Among Us Is Wise?

Now that we have considered the benefits of sacred history to inspire hope and form moral consciousness, we must also identify its unfortunate underside. Rather than explain evil and injustice, sacred histories can also enable or excuse evil and injustice. Sacred histories are selective histories. They provide partial truths and thus only partial explanations. Looking back over time through this sort of historical kaleidoscope may present beautiful and symmetrical images of the past. History, however, is anything but neat. Life is anything but logical. More complicated explanations of injustice are often left out of the story. Inexplicable tragedies are glibly explained.

Recall the people we desire to see in the biblical text. We want to use the lenses of love to see those whom God sees, those on the margins or rendered otherwise invisible. David and Solomon's moral failings are insufficient justifications for the social miseries associated with exile experienced by the most vulnerable of Israel. Moreover, David's affair with Bathsheba could never explain his daughter Tamar's rape by her half-brother Amnon (2 Sam. 13:1–14).

We can make similar comments about the narrative intended to explain Solomon's good fortune. Sacred history locates God as the source of Solomon's immense wealth and wisdom. Because Solomon asked God for wisdom, God gave him what he asked for and more. A more expansive history of the nation under Solomon's rule might also consider the ways increased taxation on the people contributed to Solomon's financial success and subsidized his lavish building projects. A more inclusive history would not ignore the unjust and exploitative economic system in Israel that hurt many peasants in favor of a supernatural tale of God's provision that benefited Solomon. And a more nuanced history would reveal that even the thing that caused some to revere Solomon—his wisdom—is also the very thing that caused others to view the king with suspicion and derision. One does not need to be a biblical specialist to come to this conclusion. When immense wealth concentrates at the top of any economic order, there will invariably be those who suffer at the bottom.

The Wisdom literature of the Hebrew Bible can provide some insight here. There was a robust professional class of sages in ancient Israel that most likely produced and edited the earliest forms of Wisdom literature, such as the books of Proverbs and Ecclesiastes. For the most part, Wisdom literature consisted of personal and familial teachings meant to shape moral life. They were like myths and sacred histories in this regard. Wisdom teachings sought to develop personal character while responding to and explaining the inexplicable. But unlike myths and sacred history, Wisdom literature often took the form of aphorisms, short sayings that contain accepted truth. Think Proverbs 1:7: "The fear of the Lord is the beginning of knowledge; fools despise wisdom and instruction."

Many in the professional guild of Israel regarded Solomon as their inspiration, the wisest of the wise. Whether this was the case or an example of the king's team of wise men brown-nosing their boss, we will never know. Still, much of the Wisdom literature is written in Solomon's name. Israel's sacred history provides the narrative account of Solomon's wisdom, and the Wisdom literature puts it on display. If 2 Samuel offers Solomon's spiritual biography, the book of Proverbs is a book of "quotable quotes" from Solomon's folk wisdom.

The Wisdom literature, particularly the books of Proverbs and Ecclesiastes, captures much of the moral meaning of the Dynastic literature in concise phrases. For these reasons, I read the Wisdom literature as an extension of the Dynastic literature. They complement one another to serve as a message to reinforce the social ideals and assumed virtues that many people take for granted. Like sacred histories, these moral teachings can have both positive and negative effects.

For example, if folk wisdom teaches that a lazy hand causes poverty but hard workers get rich (Prov. 10:3), then it only makes sense to believe that the poor have brought their suffering upon themselves. If conventional wisdom teaches that physical impairments such as blindness, illness, or the inability to walk render one unworthy to offer sacrifice in the temple (Lev. 21:18), then it only makes sense that their presence would be devalued in the larger society. And if it is the convention to believe that suffering is a result of sin, then, of course, a besieged nation will lay the blame for military conquest at their own feet, if not at the doorstep of God.

This is what I mean when I suggest that sacred history can both enable and excuse evil and injustice. When sacred history extends conventional wisdom into narrative form, the stories people tell themselves to explain reality often miss the mark. Like the proverbs that speak to the issues of poverty, physical impairment, and the source of suffering, life's complicated questions receive overly simplistic answers. So-called wisdom becomes a butcher knife that cuts carelessly and bluntly.

This manipulation of wisdom was not lost on those in the ancient world. As David Penchansky argues in *Understanding Wisdom Literature: Conflict and Dissonance in the Hebrew Text*, some storytellers and writers were aware of the power imbalance and skeptical of those who celebrated wisdom's pursuit. These subversive writers regarded wisdom as a two-sided coin with a dangerous underside. What might be a tool of humble service for one could be a method of social control and domination for another. There is a fine line between humility and vanity, a short path between noble administration and shrewd manipulation.

Let us look at examples where the ancients rejected wisdom as a noble category and challenged theodicies that offered pat explanations of the exile. We can start with the prophets. Both Isaiah (eighth century BCE) and Jeremiah (sixth century BCE) criticize wisdom. Calling into question an alliance between the nation and Egypt to offset a threat from the Assyrians, Isaiah 31:1–2 reads,

> Alas for those who go down to Egypt for help
> and who rely on horses,
> who trust in chariots because they are many
> and in horsemen because they are very strong
> but do not look to the Holy One of Israel
> or consult the Lord! Yet he too is wise and brings disaster.

Likewise, there is a blistering critique of the sage class in Jeremiah 8:8–9:

> How can you say, "We are wise,
> and the law of the Lord is with us,"
> when, in fact, the false pen of the scribes
> has made it into a lie?
> The wise shall be put to shame,
> they shall be dismayed and taken;
> since they have rejected the word of the Lord,
> what wisdom is in them?

The prophets thought the explanations of suffering by the so-called wise men were insufficient and that their justifications were inappropriate. Thus, we can turn to the prophets for a more robust and precise explanation for the suffering of the people. By most historical accounts, the eighth-century BCE prophet Amos was a political and religious outsider. From the southern kingdom of Judah, he condemned the northern rulers for their willingness to "sell the righteous for silver, and the needy for a pair of sandals—they who trample the head of the poor into the dust, and push the afflicted out of the way" (Amos 2:6–7).

There is also an alternative way to read the gruesome account of Amnon raping his sister Tamar. Rather than this being a sort of divine retribution on David's household in return for the father's sins, it is possible to view this narrative as an account against the sages. In devising a plan to seize Tamar, Amnon reached out to his cousin Jonadab. The writer of this text describes Jonadab as "very wise," and it is Jonadab who concocts the plan that enables Amnon to overtake Tamar. Hence, the writer places those who consider themselves wise, possibly the class of sages themselves, as the source of such evil as rape. Tamar's body becomes a metaphor for an exploited people, manipulated by the wiles of those who dispense wisdom on behalf of the wealthy and powerful.

## Waving a Fist at God

To follow through with the expressed aims of this book, let's take an empathetic and morally imaginative approach in dealing with this question of theodicy. How should we as people of faith make sense of suffering and injustice in our world? Fortunately, the Hebrew Bible in general and the Wisdom literature in particular already provide us with a fantastic start in the book of Job.

The book of Job ought to be read in its entirety. The book describes Job as a righteous man who is blameless and upright before God. He is wealthy. He has a beautiful family. He is a man of honor. Thus, the link between Job's moral righteousness and personal prosperity is self-evident. This is why Satan decides he wants to challenge God by exposing what he believes to be Job's disingenuous piety. What follows is a wager between God and Satan involving the health, wealth, and family of Job that might remind one of the powerful pronouncement from the Earl of Gloucester in William Shakespeare's *King Lear:* "As flies to wanton boys are we to the gods. They kill us for sport."

Second, all credible secondary sources identify the book of Job as a moral tale that wrestles with the question of theodicy. The story offers competing responses to the problem of evil and injustice in the form of Job's three friends who visit the protagonist. Though they assemble to comfort Job, they only contribute to his suffering. For in these friends we witness the traditional responses to suffering. They argue that God is just and God's judgments are always right, so obviously there is an unconfessed sin that Job needs to own. Job's sin, then, is the source of his suffering, which includes the loss of his property, the death of his ten children, and having his body afflicted with leprosy.

Third, we must consider what we bring to the text. Certainly, the book of Job speaks to us in various ways based on personal circumstances. Yet even those who have never read the book of Job will find such an account all too tragic and familiar. For instance, this is a storyline that I have witnessed numerous times when sitting with individuals or families where tragedy has struck. Whether it's the death of a child, a bleak diagnosis from a doctor, or a terrible natural disaster that scars property and psyche, I cringe every time a well-meaning Christian shows up with a feckless explanation on behalf of God. "We know that everything happens for a reason," some say. "Maybe God decided that he needed your baby in heaven more than you do on earth," is another jarring response. And eventually, someone will get around to the most thoughtless theodicy of them all: "It is okay. God does not make mistakes." Like Job's friends, some of us are amazingly quick to provide trite and cliché responses to another person's pain—responses that are particularly insensitive since they all too often set a person's grief in opposition to their faith.

Such boilerplate responses may reveal more about our fears than they do about our faith. They may speak to our need for the comfort and security of a rational world that adheres to the simple facts of life—a world that is entirely different from an uncomfortable, insecure, and irrational world that demands we search long and hard for the deeper truths of our existence. Hebrew Bible scholar Carol Newsom argues in *The Book of Job: A Contest of Moral Imaginations* that our passion for moral order is a desire for security and power. We would rather sound certain while speaking in ignorance than acknowledge the truth of life's uncertainty. Some of us are even willing to blame ourselves when evil strikes rather than make peace with the possibility of life's circumstances.

I encounter so many students who prove this point when trying to account for tragedy: "If I had only been there, my father wouldn't have died." "I knew I should not have let my roommate go on that trip." When given a choice, many of us prefer feelings of guilt over feelings of powerlessness. We take false comfort in insufficient explanations and misdirected responsibility rather than admit that there are some things in life that we will never understand. This is the moral message found in the book of Job.

Finally, when we sit down inside of the narrative and put on the lenses of love, who do we see? Traditionally, Job is the hero of the story. His herculean response to tragedy has secured his place in literary history as a paragon of patience and devotion to God. Even some of the most repeated lines of the Christian faith extend from Job passing God's test. There is the line of pious resignation to life's circumstances: "The Lord gave, and the Lord has taken away: blessed be the name of the Lord" (Job 1:21). There is the powerful proclamation of enduring trust in God: "Though he slay me, yet will I trust in him" (13:15 KJV). And there is Job's rebuke, in response to his wife who is positioned as a theological foil when she tells Job to curse God and die: "Shall we receive the good at the hand of God, and not receive the bad?" (2:10).

The problem with these more traditional interpretations of the story is twofold. For one, some of us may have a problem relating to Job. We wish that we could handle the trials of life with his resolve and stoic nature, but most likely we will just be lying to ourselves and others by repeating popular though insincere biblical quotes. We pretend to have the patience of Job on the outside, while our hearts are breaking on the inside. Second, those who succeed in living up to Job's response to tragedy can often be less sympathetic to the suffering of those around them. Rather than empathize with others and provide comfort, we might follow Job's lead and just tell others to "suck it up" as a sign of our faith and professed moral superiority. In the process, we imagine ourselves emulating Job, yet we become another version of the comforters in the story.

This is why, in my view, Job is not the person who gives the most sympathetic response to suffering in the text. To the contrary, when I look around in the story for the most vulnerable character, I find it in the person of Job's wife. We do not know her name or anything about her background. We just know that she has received a bad rap in theological history. She was placed in the text as a prop—a symbol of bad faith—rather than as a person. What does it mean to read the story through her eyes rather than privileging Job's suffering alone? To see the world through her eyes is to learn something about her suffering.

She lost ten children. That is about ninety months of life that developed in her womb, and ten mouths that nursed from her breasts. She witnessed the family fortune disappear. That renders a woman even more vulnerable as a future impoverished widow. And she had to sit by day after day and watch her husband deteriorate due to the effects of a deadly disease. Most of us know that the only thing more tragic than facing down a chronic illness or terrible disease is the thought of having to witness your life partner suffer. This is the reason that most people pray the selfish but loving prayer that they might die before their spouse. When we look at the situation through her eyes, we might have more sympathy for this woman who looked upon her dying husband's body and declared, "Please, honey. Just curse God and die."

This sentiment is neither blasphemous nor a demonstrated lack of faith. For those who have endured extreme injustice and been subjected to unspeakable suffering, to fight with God can feel like the only possible response, the only possible demonstration of piety. In the face of the Holocaust, Jewish theologians had to find a way to reconcile their anger and pain with their sustained commitment to God. They found it in what they called a theodicy of protest. This view of suffering rejects all explanations of evil and injustice while refusing to make excuses for God. A theodicy of protest realizes that a willingness to challenge and even curse God is a radical affirmation of one's faith in God.

Nobel Prize winner and Holocaust survivor Elie Wiesel illustrates this in his book *A Jew Today*. Wiesel narrates the story of a Jewish family sent into exile during the reign of King Ferdinand and Isabel for refusing to adopt the Christian faith. The man, his wife, and their two children try to make their way across an endless desert. All of them fall asleep one night, but only three wake up the next morning. The father digs a grave for his wife and proceeds to recite a hymn of praise known as the Kaddish. The next day the father loses his older son, and he proceeds to responds the same way. The night, when the surviving son passes on, the man digs another grave and prays to God:

> Master of the Universe, I know what You want—I understand what You are doing. You want despair to overwhelm me. You want me to cease believing in You, to cease praying to You, to cease invoking Your name to glorify and sanctify it. Well, I tell you: No, no—a thousand times no! You shall not succeed! In spite of me and in spite of You, I shall shout the Kaddish, which is a song of faith, for You and against You. This song You shall not still, God of Israel.

**For Further Reading**

Clifford, Richard. *The Wisdom Literature*. Interpreting Biblical Texts. Nashville: Abingdon Press, 1998.

Esler, Philip F., ed. *Ancient Israel: The Old Testament in Its Social Context*. Minneapolis: Fortress Press, 2005.

Esler, Philip F. *Sex, Wives, and Warriors: Reading Biblical Narrative with Its Ancient Audience*. Eugene, OR: Cascade Books, 2011.

Gutierrez, Gustavo. *On Job: God-Talk and the Suffering of the Innocent*. Maryknoll, NY: Orbis Books, 1987.

Kushner, Harold S. *When Bad Things Happen to Good People*. 20th anniversary ed. New York: Schocken Books, 2001.

Newsom, Carol A. *The Book of Job: A Contest of Moral Imaginations*. New York: Oxford University Press, 2003.

Townes, Emilie. *Troubling in My Soul: Womanist Perspectives on Evil and Suffering*. Maryknoll, NY: Orbis Books, 2015.

# 5

## Origins, Apologies, and Attacks

### Political Allegory in the Pentateuch

> If you live today you breathe in nihilism. . . . It's the gas
> you breathe. If I hadn't had the Church to fight it with or
> to tell me the necessity of fighting it, I would be the stink-
> ingest logical positivist you ever saw right now.
> —Flannery O'Connor

> He who controls the past controls the future. He who
> controls the present controls the past.
> —George Orwell

#### Sacred History as Political Allegory

Now that my twins are in middle school, one of my joys in life is
reading great literature with them. I can think of no better way
to ignite our imaginations and expand our moral imaginations
than embarking on literary voyages in tales such as *Lord of the
Flies*, *A Raisin in the Sun*, and the Hunger Games series. They
inspire lively conversations about fear of the other and about
racial, economic, and gender-related injustice. Each uncovers
life's constant battle between hope and disappointment.

Recently I read George Orwell's 1945 classic, *Animal Farm*, with my daughter. The story is about farm animals, inspired by a revolutionary old boar and calculating pigs, who decide that it is time to break free of the shackles of human oppression and exploitation. Mr. Jones, the landowner and farmer, is cast off of the land, and the animals systematize their vision of equality into a philosophy they call "animalism." Nevertheless, hierarchies develop among the animals over time. Pigs become the decision makers as horses and cows labor with little input. All the while, the cunning and conniving pigs move into Farmer Jones's house, begin wearing his clothes, and embody the worst of his previous practices. The pigs do this, of course, while saying to the other animals repeatedly, "This is what is best. Besides, you don't want Mr. Jones back, do you?"

*Animal Farm* is a fable that thinly veils a blistering political critique. Orwell penned this tale as an allegorical account of the Russian Revolution. The author's mythic uprising by the animals and their subsequent autocratic rule attacks the brutal dictatorship of Joseph Stalin and the implementation of Stalinism in the Soviet Union. Propaganda producing pigs, workhorses turned beasts of burden, and slogan-chanting sheep represent the essential components of any unjust political structures that tout equality. More importantly for our purposes here, the genre of *Animal Farm* is an excellent example of the stories found in the Pentateuch, the first five books of the Hebrew Bible.

As children, many of us listened to stories and sang songs derived from the Pentateuch. If you attended Sunday school or Vacation Bible School, I am confident that you learned about animals marching two-by-two onto Noah's ark, sang the song "Father Abraham had many sons, and many sons had Father Abraham," colored pictures of baby Moses being rescued from the Nile, and acted out skits in which the children of Israel cross a divided Red Sea to escape Pharaoh's army.

The Pentateuch holds a special place among both Jews and Christians. Jews refer to these books—Genesis, Exodus, Leviticus, Numbers, and Deuteronomy—as the *Torah*, the Hebrew word meaning "to guide or teach." Christians call these first books of the Old Testament the *Pentateuch* after the Greek for "five scrolls." Both Jews and Christians alike refer to them as the books of the Law. This latter characterization has much to do with the large sections of the Pentateuch dedicated to providing laws, statutes, and commands from God.

Referring to the first five books of the Hebrew Bible as the Law, however, can be somewhat misleading. These books are so much more than a mere transcription of laws. They provide a mythic account of God's promise, the people's trials, and then God's liberation of the people and ultimate fulfillment of that pledge. A summary of the entire narrative is found in Deuteronomy 26:5–9:

> A wandering Aramean was my ancestor; he went down into Egypt and lived there as an alien, few in number, and there he became a great nation, mighty and populous. When the Egyptians treated us harshly and afflicted us, by imposing hard labor on us, we cried to the Lord, the God of our ancestors; the Lord heard our voice and saw our affliction, our toil, and our oppression. The Lord brought us out of Egypt with a mighty hand and an outstretched arm, with a terrifying display of power, and with signs and wonders; and he brought us into this place and gave us this land, a land flowing with milk and honey.

This grand tale of faith, failure, and ultimate redemption is why so many generations and diverse peoples identify with the children of Israel. The Pentateuch's engaging narratives and dramatic moral lessons concerning patience, sin, and forgiveness provide a mold for communities to shape themselves.

As in previous chapters, our first aim should be to identify how we ought to read the stories of the Pentateuch. The Pentateuch is similar to the Dynastic literature insofar as we should approach its stories as sacred history. Unlike with the Dynastic literature, independent sources do not provide us with the same kind of corroborating details about the period from Abraham to Moses that we have about the period from Israel's monarchy to the Babylonian exile. Based on the extensive archaeological research conducted in the region, one could reasonably expect scientists to have uncovered some evidence if many of the events in the Pentateuch had taken place. Tales of the patriarchs are most likely literary fiction. Thus, we should concern ourselves more with the truths of the Pentateuch than the facts of its history.

Many stories of the Pentateuch developed into their current form over the course of centuries. The myths began as oral narratives that ultimately became a part of the written tradition roughly between 1000 and 500 BCE. The actual writings that we read as Scripture are widely believed to have been recorded during Persian control over the region, between 538 and 332 BCE.[1] The Pentateuch provides tales and legends as veiled social and political commentaries on the nation of Israel, its neighbors, and its enemies. Biblical writers use such allegory—which is essentially an extended metaphor—to defend and defame figures in Israel's history as well as to justify

---

1. There are few biblical scholars who would deny the importance of the exile in compiling the sources of the Pentateuch, although there remain important voices such as Richard Elliott Friedman and William Henry Propp who hold on to an earlier dating of sources (around the ninth century BCE). See Richard Elliott Friedman, *The Exile and Biblical Narrative: The Formation of the Deuteronomistic and Priestly Works*, Harvard Semitic Monographs (Chico, CA: Scholars Press, 1981); and William Henry Propp, *Exodus 1–18: A New Translation with Introduction and Commentary*, Anchor Bible (New York: Doubleday, 1999). I find more convincing the arguments that locate the completion of Israel's sacred history in the Pentateuch during the exilic period of the sixth century. This is not to suggest that stories were not in circulation, particularly in oral form, for centuries prior to the exile. But there is ample reason to take a more conservative approach and date the writing of the Pentateuch later. For anyone interested in delving deeper in these debates, there are some wonderful resources available. In my own research, I have found few books as helpful as John Van Seters, *The Pentateuch: A Social-Science Commentary*, Trajectories (Sheffield: Sheffield Academic Press, 1999); and Joel S. Baden, *The Composition of the Pentateuch: Renewing the Documentary Hypothesis*, Anchor Yale Bible Reference Library (New Haven, CT: Yale University Press, 2012).

or critique the political establishment. As in Orwell's *Animal Farm*, all is not as it appears.

Great literary fiction underscores important truths. As expected, many storylines in the Pentateuch bear witness to the character of God. Also, stories introduce individual heroes and villains devised to extol or indict entire tribes or nations. Appearing as little more than dysfunctional family conflicts, some stories prove to be social instructions on how the government ought to interpret previous or contemporary political developments. Rabbi David Sperling of Hebrew Union College in New York argues that myths of the Pentateuch are easily read as political allegories of the ancient world. Characters such as Abraham, Jacob, and Moses represent political leaders such as Saul, David, and Solomon. Ancient storytellers encoded messages about their political leaders within narratives about revered ancestors.

This claim may be difficult for some to fathom. Many reject any relationship between church and state in the contemporary United States, as the traditional view is that religion and politics do not, or at least should not, mix. This explains why when we clergy weigh in from our pulpits on matters of climate change, economic inequality, or gun violence, there is always a contingent of the faithful who will describe us as being "too political." That sort of an impenetrable wall dividing religion from politics, education, and business, however, is a modern phenomenon. There is no word for "religion" in biblical Hebrew, since the Hebrew people never conceived of religious practices and religious faith standing alone as a concept independent of other social, political, or economic interactions. Hence, I am comfortable claiming that by the time many of the oral traditions, legends, and sacred myths were transcribed in the Pentateuch, they had taken on explicit theological purposes, social agendas, and political aims. The more we are receptive to reading the Pentateuch with a fuller sense of its original intentions in its world, the better we may begin to apply Scripture ethically and morally in our world.

There are at least three major types of allegorical myths found in the Pentateuch. Some myths explain how certain aspects of society came into existence. This type of origin myth, called an **etiology**, identifies causes to explain some aspect of our current reality. Some myths are apologetic. Apologetic myths defend the character of an individual or group. And some myths are polemical. Polemical myths discredit a person or group. All three of these types had a wide array of motives, but they all can shed light on the various worldviews representative of ancient Israel.

### Fighting Wars with Words

Let's begin with one of the most famous origin accounts in history, the etiology of Adam and Eve. Although no one can identify when and where the original myth developed in its earlier oral forms, ancient Israelites likely shaped this story to explain a shift from a nomadic hunter-gatherer lifestyle to a sedentary agricultural lifestyle. In one of the more accessible books on biblical interpretation, *How to Read the Bible,* James Kugel provides a compelling reading of this creation myth that encourages agrarian dependency to labor and land.

Farming a single plot of land was an arduous responsibility that demanded long, taxing hours in the sun. Shifts from a nomadic to a settled agrarian approach coincided with viewing childbirth through a model of planting and harvest. Land settlement demanded a new level of responsibility from men and women to their sexual partner and offspring. No longer could one believe that babies simply appeared, or those nomadic men could just keep roaming to the next region. Agricultural dependency and paternal awareness inaugurated a new social order in which a man would cling to his wife and become one flesh with her (Gen. 2:24). And just as a man had to toil and labor in the fields for his livelihood, a woman had to bear the burden of toil and suffering in delivering children—future laborers for the land. With the agricultural model of property cultivation at the time, this may explain why women became regarded as part of a man's property. A woman belonged only to her husband, as God in the story explains: "In pain you shall bring forth children, yet your desire shall be for your husband, and he shall rule over you" (Gen. 3:16).

The allegory emphasizes the idea that God ordained toil and tending. It is narrative evidence that a man's responsibility is to the land and a woman's responsibility is to men. Thus, the insistence on Adam's responsibility and Eve's dependency makes this creation account a useful allegory to underscore the pervasiveness of gender-based honor. The allegory of Adam and Eve shames men and women into what was deemed their socially appropriate roles at the time.

This theme of gender-based honor continues in the lives of the patriarchs and matriarchs in Genesis 12–50. The fulfillment of God's promise to Abraham is directly related to his heir's capacity to live up to this standard of honor. Hence, we see patriarchs concerned with having the "right" woman, as is the case with the love triangle between Abraham, Sarah, and Hagar, and with Jacob's bizarre marriages to sisters Rachel and Leah. Matriarchs had to ensure that the "right" son was heir to the promise, as seen in competitions between Ishmael and Isaac, as well as between Jacob and Esau. Before one can make this critical choice, of course, one must first have children. Therefore, overcoming barrenness is a common theme among the matriarchs and patriarchs. These sorts of allegories, then, not only provided storytellers an opportunity to insert God's power into the story, but they demonstrated how the Hebrew people extended from an honorable history and how they, too, could be blessed well into the future if they lived similarly noble lives of sacrifice and submission. One can imagine that this was an important point for Hebrews living in exile or under foreign rule.

As some stories were etiologic accounts of origins for the nation, apologetic accounts were told to defend certain behaviors, namely, of beloved political figures. Israel's leaders had propaganda agents that today's elected officials would pay top dollar to hire. These storytellers crafted characters that could foreshadow and defend the behaviors of adored leaders such as King David and King Jeroboam.

Consider the character Abraham (at times referred to as Abram in Genesis). Abraham's existence cannot be proved with current archaeological or historical data. What we do know from archaeological discoveries in Egypt, though, is that a tribal group early in the thirteenth century BCE named Raham lived in the territory later called the kingdom of Israel. A common practice for a Hebrew storyteller was to designate an elder of the tribe. *Ab-Raham* would mean "father of the Raham." Hence, it would not be a huge leap for this name to have remained in cultural lore and been appropriated and redeployed in numerous songs, poems, and legends. What is known is that at some point Abraham became an allegorical archetype used to symbolize significant events of the nation and prominent historical figures.

Genesis 14 offers an illustrative allegory featuring Abraham. Far from being an elderly, pious man of faith, Abraham is described in this chapter as a valiant warrior and intimidating diplomat. A war is raging. Four tribes from outside Canaan are fighting to help liberate four areas in the region: Sodom, Gomorrah, Admah, and Zeboiim. (According to sacred history, these latter four areas are each eventually considered wicked and destroyed by God.) Abraham's nephew Lot is living in Sodom and is captured by the enemy. Abraham enlists his men to help Sodom and to deliver Lot. When Sodom's king attempts to pay Abraham with the spoils of war, Abraham offers the most honorable response one can imagine: "I have sworn to the Lord, God Most High, maker of heaven and earth, that I would not take a thread or a sandal-thong or anything that is yours, so that you might not say, 'I have made Abram rich'" (Gen. 14:22–23). Abraham refuses anything for himself but only asks to provide the appropriate share for the men who fought alongside him.

Genesis 14 is an apologetic account intended to defend the reputation of King David. The writings of the prophets reveal that not all in Israel looked well upon David's military exploits. Yes, David's military acumen expanded the borders and led to a period of national security. But this period also enriched the throne financially, a cause of concern for many during David's day. Consider the parallels between Abraham in Genesis 14 and the story of David reluctantly entering battle in 1 Samuel 30. The Amalekites raid David's camp in Ziklag. Though the men grumble against David and even consider stoning him, the story says that David is not willing to pursue the Amalekites until he spends time in prayer, inquiring about the Lord's will. After receiving encouragement from God, David chases the raiding party, discovers their location, and overtakes them. Four hundred soldiers are with David, with another two hundred too fatigued to fight. David and his men come back with everything that the Amalekites stole from them. Although the soldiers have already designated the reclaimed goods as "David's spoil," David returns everything to the soldiers, even to the two hundred too fatigued to join him in battle.

The parallels between the Abrahamic account in Genesis 14 and the Davidic account in 1 Samuel 30 seem to establish Abraham as a moral archetype for David. Abraham reluctantly enters the fray to help deliver his nephew Lot and others from the enemy. Similarly, David selflessly and reluctantly enters the battle to reclaim family members and property that were seized illegally. Abraham refuses to accept a reward for his help but only asks for allies to compensate his men. David redistributes all of the stolen property to his troops, although the soldiers declared it the property of the king. The story demonstrates that David possesses the same moral character as the nation's founding father Abraham. Not only is David thoughtful and prayerful before entering a conflict, when he does fight, it is to defend the honor of others rather than for personal gain.

Similar to the ways allegories used Abraham to defend the honor of David, other patriarchs were employed to defend the inaugural leader of the northern kingdom of Israel, Jeroboam. The stories of the patriarch Jacob in Genesis 28 and 32 authorize Jeroboam's claims to the throne. Take the account of what is commonly referred to as "Jacob's ladder." While Jacob sleeps, God drops a ladder from heaven with angels ascending and descending. God reiterates the promise to Jacob that his descendants will be numerous and blessed. When he wakes, Jacob erects an altar and names the site Bethel, which means "house of God."

The story of Jacob's ladder may serve as a prequel to the account of Jeroboam and the northern kingdom seceding from the house of David in 1 Kings 12. The Kings account depicts Jeroboam as anxious about the people's possible return to Jerusalem to offer sacrifices, believing that they might reunite with the southern kingdom and observe Rehoboam's rule. So Jeroboam erects two calves of gold and places the priests in Bethel to oversee newly established festivals similar to those in Judah. He provides a spiritual alternative to returning to Jerusalem. While 1 Kings 12 portrays Jeroboam's actions as cynical, defensive, and even sinful, Genesis 28 makes the subtle case that Jeroboam was simply reinstituting what Jacob had already established. Bethel was the true house of God.

Along with etiologies that describe origins and apologies that defend character, there are polemical accounts intended to slander. The Pentateuch is full of print "hit jobs." Sacred histories were written about the past to indict political leaders of the present.

Let's stick with the politically polarizing figure of Jeroboam. There were contrasting stories about Jeroboam's reign. If the story of Jacob's ladder was meant to authorize Israel's leader, one might suspect that writings from the southern kingdom sought to discredit Jeroboam. In 1 Kings 12, for instance, Jeroboam establishes new sites of worship to offer sacrifices.

He creates two calves of gold to represent God. This is in keeping with archaeological finds in northern Israel. The bull was a symbol of strength in the ancient Near East; thus, to see a gold bull at a place of worship would be as common as seeing a large gold pipe organ in a sanctuary today. It was part of the religious decor.

The story told in Exodus 32, however, would have us believe otherwise. This chapter contains obvious parallels to 1 Kings 12. God has delivered the children of Israel from Egyptian bondage, and they are making their way to the land that God promised. God calls Moses to the top of Mount Sinai to provide instruction, and the people begin to grumble and complain. They approach Aaron and say to him, "Come, make gods for us, who shall go before us; as for this Moses, the man who brought us up out of the land of Egypt, we do not know what has become of him." Aaron commands the people to bring him all of their gold rings and earrings, which he melts in order to make a golden calf. And in language that is pulled directly from 1 Kings 12, Aaron declares, "These are your gods, O Israel, who brought you up out of the land of Egypt!" Aaron then proceeds to institute a new festival and offer burnt offerings at this site—an apparent mocking of Jeroboam.

In both religious and nonreligious circles, the image of a golden calf has become the most convenient and recognizable metaphor for idolatry. Thus, one might say that the southern kingdom of Judah won this storytelling battle. The writers of Exodus 32 transformed an otherwise innocuous symbol into the most recognized symbol of idolatry. What was an accepted symbol of strength in the ancient world is now a symbol of people's sin in our world. Stories have power.

### Reclaiming the Garden

So now that we have considered the ways communities in the ancient world may have heard the stories of the Pentateuch, we can examine how some of these same stories translate for our world. We will use the three interrelated steps discussed in chapters 2 and 3. First, we immerse ourselves in the story with critical minds and sensitive hearts and with knowledge of the social customs and hierarchies of power in the text. This allows us to empathize with characters who are most vulnerable in the narrative. Second, we identify historically appropriate connections from the ancient world to our modern world. These connections are less literal and more symbolic. Those of us in twenty-first-century America do not have a king like David or Solomon, but we can consider the behaviors of the executive, legislative, and judicial branches of government. Third, we use moral imaginations to envision a world that is more inclusive, loving, and just than the one we currently inhabit. This is our bold attempt to see characters and social structures in the text as God might see them, through the lenses of love and compassion.

Let's revisit the creation account in the garden of Eden. Our earlier findings suggest that the creation account of Adam and Eve promotes responsibility and accountability—responsibility for cultivating the land and accountability to one's family. These are important and valuable themes. They reflect what it means to be a mature moral agent: all of us must be held responsible for our actions as well as accountable to the larger communities in which we live.

Nevertheless, this creation account as written, and as it is conventionally taught, convey features of the story that belie human equality. What happens to Eve? Any notion of human equality is eclipsed by patriarchal honor and female submission. In its original context, women and children are considered extensions of physical property, and therefore forced into lives of dependency under male authority. Such views are wholly unacceptable in principle and in practice.

As a matter of principle, I cannot affirm that humanity represents the image of God and also declare that some human beings ought to have authority over others due to factors such as gender, race, ethnicity, or religion. This contradicts the

principle of human dignity and cuts against the inherent equal
value of all people. We are either all equal in the eyes of God
or not. I have the audacity to believe that we are. The principle
of human equality under God is not a cliché phrase for me. It
is a sincere theological commitment.

As a matter of practice, such a view of female subjection
under male authority is not concurrent with the economic realities of most American households. Over the past forty years,
dual incomes have proven to be a life vest for keeping middle-
class families afloat in an increasingly stratified economy. By the
sweat of women's faces, as well as men's, bread has remained
on many tables. Women also tend to assume a greater chunk of
childcare responsibilities and domestic chores. Since women
are more likely to earn college degrees than men, and female-
dominated careers such as registered nurses, home health and
personal care aides, and office clerks have the highest pro-
jected growth potential over the next decade, theologies that
subject women to male authority are as impractical as they are
unjust. It would thus seem appropriate for more Adams to take
responsibility for making sure that the Eves are earning equal
pay for equal work.

Speaking of pay, this is a second area where we might consider this creation story for our contemporary context. The
ancients emphasized the importance of labor and toil because
it meant survival for early agrarians. God affirms the virtue
and honor of work from the very outset of creation. What does
it mean, then, when men and women are denied a just share
of prosperity because in many areas full-time work does not
equate to a decent basic standard of living? Does our society
show that it honors the dignity of labor, as God did in Eden,
when all too often the minimum wage keeps people trapped
below the poverty line?

Much of this has to do with unequal growth in the United
States economy over the past forty years. In the final quarter of the previous century, the United States experienced

technological innovations, market transformation, and political deregulations that impelled seismic shifts in the nation's political economy. Changes in advanced forms of cybertechnologies, computation, and telecommunication drastically changed the way information spreads and how goods and services are created and exchanged throughout the globe. Computerization replaced human manufacturing and transformed the service sector. This proved a pyrrhic victory for the masses, since these developments boosted production and profits while eradicating millions of well-paid, blue-collar union jobs and midlevel service providers.

This postindustrial change spurred the globalization of capital markets and a cheap, seemingly inexhaustible labor pool. As Douglass Massey writes so elegantly and passionately in his book *Categorically Unequal: The American Stratification System*, American workers "found themselves competing in a global hiring hall that pitted them against billions of ambitious but much poorer workers in the developing world." Taken together, such technological and market shifts led to a rise in the unequal distribution of wealth in America toward the top 10 percent of income earners.

Many of us know the statistics well. The richest 10 percent control three-quarters of American wealth. And gains were even greater among the most elite. According to a report released by Oxfam International in anticipation of the World Economic Forum, 82 percent of all global wealth created in 2017 went to the top 1 percent. The bottom 50 percent of the world's population saw no increase in wealth. If 1 percent of the garden's inhabitants lay claim to and hoard such a large percent of resources, our nation looks far less like God's Eden and more like Orwell's Animal Farm.

How ought the Christian church respond to such economic injustice? Is there a word from the Lord? How else might this commonly referenced creation narrative of Adam and Eve speak to our current economic reality?

## Mourning at the Red Sea

Another favorite tale from the Pentateuch is the Exodus narrative. The book of Exodus details the dramatic saga of how God hears the cries of God's people, enslaved in Egypt for four hundred years. God raises up a deliverer named Moses, a Hebrew who had the privilege of being raised in the palace of Pharaoh after his mother protected him from genocide. Despite this relative privilege, Moses as an adult could not ignore the pain and suffering of his people under the whips of Pharaoh. A showdown takes place, as Moses stands before Pharaoh and declares, "Let my people go!" In response to Pharaoh's hardened heart, God sends plagues upon Egypt, and Pharaoh agrees to release the Hebrew people. Pharaoh makes one last-ditch effort to send his army after them. This showdown at the Red Sea takes place in Exodus 14. The story creates the conditions for God to demonstrate to the people God's power and might. God tells Moses to stretch his hand across the Red Sea, and God sends a wind all night long to blow the sea back, enabling the people to walk across on dry ground.

After checking multiple secondary sources, I discovered a few factual holes in this legend. Scholars are in consensus that the Israelites were never enslaved in Egypt. Historians and archaeologists are clear: if a large group of people from Canaan, a region in western Asia, resided in Egypt for generations, some evidence would have remained. The cultural differences between this North African empire and Canaan were distinct enough that such a mass immigration would have left a historical impression. Not to mention, if the greatest empire of the day had been brought to its knees by an enslaved people inside of its own borders, there would be historical evidence.

There is evidence that the Hebrew people were enslaved to the mighty empire at some point while living in the land of Canaan. It seems that the exodus story developed over time as God's people wanted to affirm their distinctiveness from other inhabitants of Canaan. They developed what Harvard University

Hebrew Bible scholar Peter Machinist refers to as a "counter-identity" to the region. By developing an independent history as regional transplants, the Hebrews distinguished themselves from other people in western Asia. Thus, it makes sense to look for symbolic meanings that the story seeks to convey.

Consider the plagues that God unleashed on Pharaoh. When I was a kid, these plagues always seemed kind of random. Yet later I discovered that the plagues are full of symbolic meaning. The Egyptians considered Pharaoh to be a god, the Nile River was sacred, and the Egyptian fertility goddess Heqet had a frog's head. Therefore, the story makes a theological claim when Yahweh turns the Nile into blood, unleashes frogs throughout the nation, and turns the sun black. The God of the Hebrews is more than just caring and compassionate; he is stronger than all of the gods of Egypt. Here Yahweh is like a fresh-faced Cassius Clay knocking out heavyweight champion Sonny Liston. The God of the Hebrews could declare, like the boxer who came to be known as Muhammad Ali, "I am the greatest fighter that ever lived. I am a BAAAD MAN! I shook up the world!"

The end of the exodus legend drives this point home further. Yahweh creates a highway through the Red Sea. God is a powerful deliverer! Thus, we should not get bogged down in debates over whether God "really" split the Red Sea for an entire people to exit Egypt en masse. To do so would only cause us to get stuck in the mud like Pharaoh's army and miss the point of the story. The exodus is a theological account of an all-powerful God who can save and deliver.

Countless communities have appealed to the exodus motif during times of trial and travail. For instance, the exodus is among the most meaningful and lasting themes among African American Christians. This connection dates back to when enslaved Africans first began accepting the message of Christianity in the Americas. Africans connected their situation as enslaved beings in the Americas to the suffering and persecution of the children of Israel in Egypt. Abolitionist and Union Army spy Harriet Tubman earned the title "Moses of her people" by delivering dozens of enslaved African Americans via the Underground Railroad to a land of freedom. She went on to free over seven hundred more enslaved Americans when she became the first woman to lead a U.S. armed military expedition during the raid at Combahee Ferry, South Carolina, in 1863.

Due to these powerful examples of African Americans reading the struggle for abolition and equal rights into the United States through the exodus, I have never given much thought to any character in the text other than Moses and Yahweh. Most often I conceive of both in predictable ways. Moses has the courage, and Yahweh has the power. Something challenged this view in recent years that allowed me to see suffering on multiple sides.

The challenge began when my family attended a Passover **seder** at the home of one of my son's closest friends. A seder is the ritual feast that marks the beginning of the Jewish holiday of Passover. A beautiful celebration through storytelling and prayers, it allows our Jewish brothers and sisters to recall and reflect on the ways God intervened to deliver the Hebrews from slavery. When we were reading prayers from the Haggadah—the text that contains the seder order of service, prayers, songs, and questions—one moment stood out. During the recitation of the ten plagues, we spilled ten drops of wine with a reminder to never gloat over the death of an enemy. "They are made in the image of God just like us."

I remain admittedly surprised by the ways this prayer both rattled and convicted me. Never have I taken the story to its logical conclusion. All of the Egyptians experienced extreme suffering. Of all the times I have interpreted myself in the shoes of Moses, my moral imagination has never called me to think about the Egyptian parents who lost a son or the soldiers who died because they were following Pharaoh's orders.

Evil perpetrators and innocent victims make for memorable moral lessons, but our world is rarely so neat. Each of us is capable of good and evil, spirited activism and cold indifference. The history of group conflict would support the hypothesis that there were surely Egyptians who opposed Pharaoh's policies toward the Hebrews. Many Egyptians may have fought for abolition alongside Moses and the Hebrews. Did these Egyptians suffer the loss of their firstborn son too? Unfortunately, the history of the United States bears witness to the ways the choices of a few can have an incredible impact on so many. Injustice and evil anywhere can cause suffering and pain everywhere. The 1,113 names of the war dead engraved on the walls of the Memorial Church at Harvard University—men and women who lost their lives in World Wars I and II, Korea, and Vietnam—remind me of how choices made by people in one place can cause tragedy for families continents away.

There is one particular name on the wall of the sanctuary that caught my eye as soon as I accepted the position as the head of the Memorial Church. The name is Adolf Sannwald. He studied at Harvard Divinity School during the 1924–1925 academic year. Sannwald was a member of the German army and is listed among Harvard's war dead with the tag "enemy casualty" next to his name.

Further research on Sannwald revealed that he was much more complicated of a figure than originally thought. The Lutheran pastor and theologian was hardly a Nazi. There is evidence that Sannwald was a member of the Confessing Church, an underground Christian resistance movement that opposed Adolf Hitler and was associated with theologian Dietrich Bonhoeffer. In 1934 Sannwald published a pamphlet that repudiated Nazism's view of racial supremacy. "God did not choose his children on the basis of race," Sannwald argued. "We may not and will not confuse faith in Jesus Christ with some other faith in a religious or political world view." As the pastor of St. Mark's Church in Stuttgart, he offered shelter to fugitive Jews.

The German army drafted Sannwald in 1942. Due to his sermons that were critical of the German regime, he was not allowed to serve as a chaplain. Germany designated him a "common soldier" and sent him to the front lines in Russia. A bombing raid killed him less than a year later. Yet Sannwald did have one opportunity to preach on Easter Sunday 1943. His topic was the resurrection and collective guilt.

Sannwald's life is a tragic lesson about how the dividing line between innocence and guilt can often be too thin to attribute heroism or blame. Moreover, suffering is no respecter of person. The storms of injustice rain on the guilty and innocent alike. So whether they were Egyptian or Hebrew, all paid a terrible price for the sin of viewing one group of people as superior to another. This is why individual Egyptian claims of "I did not enslave anyone" or "I am not guilty" were irrelevant when the death angel showed up. Categories of good and evil, guilty and innocent, miss the point when we are working on behalf of social justice. This language is too individualized and interpersonal. It allows us to evade responsibility and ignore our culpability.

A better way of thinking about injustice involves whether or not we are willing to take responsibility for one another. Are we our brothers' and sisters' keepers? The writer James Baldwin put it eloquently: "I'm not interested in anybody's guilt. Guilt is a luxury that we can no longer afford. I know you didn't do it, and I didn't do it either, but I am responsible for it because I am a man and a citizen of this country and you are responsible for it, too, for the very same reason." May we imagine a world where we realize we are all responsible for injustice. If not, we may just find ourselves mourning one another at the Red Sea.

**For Further Reading**

Baden, Joel S. *The Composition of the Pentateuch: Renewing the Documentary Hypothesis*. New Haven, CT: Yale University Press, 2012.
Fretheim, Terrence E. *The Pentateuch*. Nashville: Abingdon Press, 1996.
Greenspahn, Frederick, ed. *Essential Papers on Israel and the Ancient Near East*. New York: NYU Press, 2000.
Kugel, James. *How to Read the Bible: A Guide to Scripture Then and Now*. New York: Free Press, 2007.
Sperling, S. David. *The Original Torah: The Political Intent of the Bible's Writers*. New York: NYU Press, 1998.
Van Seters, John. *The Pentateuch: A Social-Science Commentary*. 2nd ed. New York: Bloomsbury T&T Clark, 2015.

# 6

## Is God Racist and Sexist?

### Inappropriate Metaphors and Perverted Interpretations

> You can safely assume you've created God in your own image when it turns out that God hates all the same people you do.
>
> —Anne Lamott

> I imagine that one of the reasons people cling to their hates so stubbornly is because they sense, once hate is gone, they will be forced to deal with pain.
>
> —James Baldwin

#### Hate-Based Tales

The previous chapters introduced the different aims of biblical stories. Some narratives, for instance, employ allegory to explain social patterns, defend political leaders, and even demonize entire groups of people. These different aims create an interpretive problem. On the one hand, we have a sacred book that informs our faith as believers. On the other hand, this same book is full of tales that reveal ancient social arrangements and cultural battles that many of us find abhorrent.

How do we reconcile mean-spirited, even hateful, biblical

narratives with what we believe about a God who typifies love and grace? What do we do with Scripture that depicts God as a despiser of people based on their religion, tribal identity, or region of birth? How should we view a God who seems to sanction the subjugation, abuse, and even rape of women? If we follow biblical writers' descriptions of God in the ancient world, only one reasonable conclusion remains: God is sexist and racist.

No level of theological apologetics can defend God from such a claim *if* we conflate Scripture with God. Nor can we defend God from charges of ethnic supremacy and misogyny *if* we believe the Bible to be the last and final revelation of God in our world—hence, the reason why it was important for me to claim my understanding of Scripture at the outset of this book. As I stated in chapter 2, the Bible, though sacred, is neither divine nor the final word on God. The God I serve is so much bigger, better, broader, more loving, more inclusive, and more generous than any human writer could ever depict.

It is true that the Bible evokes a sense of awe and helps point us toward God. We must also acknowledge that the biases, claims to power, and political concerns of ancient communities ultimately informed what was passed down to us in Scripture. Biblical stories represent how the ancients viewed their world. Thus, the Bible served, and continues to serve, at least two purposes. It paints a picture of a God who provides comfort to the afflicted, encourages the oppressed, and is a champion of those living on the underside of empire. And it paints a picture of a God who hated all of the people whom the writers hated.

With these understandings in mind, I would like to use this chapter to consider three things. First, we will examine two particularly horrifying passages from the Pentateuch and how, tragically, they were entirely consistent with the worldview of some writers of the ancient Near East. The two stories are God's command to "utterly destroy" all of the inhabitants of the promised land in Deuteronomy 7:1–6, and Lot's offering up of his daughters to be raped by the townsmen of Sodom in

Genesis 19:1–9. More than these stories illustrate the writer's view of God, they reveal how the ancients viewed "the other." Second, I want us to consider historical and contemporary examples of what happens when we follow biblical writers down the rabbit hole of their creative narratives and hyperbolic rhetoric. We should not accept uncritically allegorical etiologies and apologies from the ancient world as prescriptions for our world. History reveals to us that this sort of approach to the Bible only leads to suffering and further injustice. These interpreters use Scripture to bruise and bludgeon rather than comfort and heal. Finally, I want to offer reading strategies that might enable us to provide viable counterreadings of problematic narratives that are more consistent with the overarching themes of love and justice.

## Hyperbole and Histrionics

Biblical writers were bold and brazen. They did not adhere to the modern disciplinary standards of historiography: they did not fear charges of academic dishonesty for plagiarism, and they were not concerned with anyone showing up with archaeological evidence or scientific discoveries that would unequivocally refute their accounts. In some ways, they were like the Eatonville, Florida, storytellers recorded in Zora Neale Hurston's *Mules and Men*. The better the "big old lie," the greater the chance that somebody just might believe it.

Let's analyze an origin story concerning the Canaanites that extends from the Noah account in Genesis 9. This tale does not include rising water, but rather a puzzling domestic dispute that takes place after the flood recedes. Noah disembarks from the ship, plants a vineyard, and becomes intoxicated from the wine. Noah's youngest son, Ham, discovers his father in a naked, inebriated stupor. Ham collects his two brothers, Shem and Japheth, who proceed to walk backward toward their father to cover up his body, after which they depart the tent in the same manner. Noah wakes up livid with Ham. The reasons are unclear, but Ham may have embarrassed Noah, whereas Shem and Japheth demonstrated discretion.

Whatever the reason, though, we witness one of the greatest overreactions in the history of parenthood. Noah curses Ham and his descendants forever. "Cursed be Canaan; lowest of slaves shall he be to his brothers." It just so happens that Ham is the father of the people who will come to be known as the Canaanites—the people who will be the children of Israel's sworn enemies and occupiers of the same land that God ultimately promises to Abraham. Thus, this story is a polemical allegory to justify the nation's disdain for and displacement of the Canaanites that will take place generations later. The Canaanites were doomed from the start. Their bloodline is cursed due to the original sin of their father, Ham. Hence, no punishment is too extreme nor treatment too harsh.

Beyond serving as a justification for how the children of Israel ought to mistrust and mistreat their neighbors, the story of Ham as the father of the Canaanites sets the stage for something even more nefarious. The cursing of the Canaanites helps to legitimate one of the most inhumane and xenophobic passages in Scripture:

> When the Lord your God brings you into the land that you are about to enter and occupy, and he clears away many nations before you—the Hittites, the Girgashites, the Amorites, the Canaanites, the Perizzites, the Hivites, and the Jebusites, seven nations mightier and more numerous than you—and when the Lord your God gives them over to you and you defeat them, then you must utterly destroy them. Make no covenant with them and show them no mercy. Do not intermarry with them, giving your daughters to their sons or taking their daughters for your sons, for that would turn away your children from following me, to serve other gods. Then the anger of the Lord would be kindled against you, and he would destroy you quickly. But this is how you must deal with them: break down their altars, smash their pillars, hew down their sacred poles, and burn their idols with fire. For

you are a people holy to the Lord your God; the Lord your God has chosen you out of all the peoples on the earth to be his people, his treasured possession. (Deut. 7:1–6)

This text is abhorrent. Its genocidal language and murderous descriptions of God cannot be justified in our time or its own. Yet the language is relatively easy to explain when one views Israel as a product of tribal culture of the ancient Near East. A sociohistorical approach would allow us to take a step back from the biblical narrative and into the world in which such a narrative was produced and thus disrupt any simplistic interpretation.

The people who came to constitute Israel emerged as a tribal coalition in the late Bronze Age (1570–1200 BCE). Tribes were largely an extension of household kinship structures that gathered into informal social networks that identified a common ancestor and/or god(s). In one instance, Ephraim may refer to the "house of Joseph," which constitutes the tribes of Ephraim and Manasseh together. This identity unit was independent of territory. Additionally, there are times that tribal identity refers to geographic territory. Tribes competed for and negotiated land like any other limited resource. Throughout the Hebrew Bible, tribes shift their associations and allegiances. For example, the tribe of Ephraim joined with King David of Judah in order to unite the kingdom of Israel. Nevertheless, the tribe eventually united with other northern tribes to support one of their own, King Jeroboam, when he broke away from Judah in order to establish the northern kingdom of Israel.

Because alliances and allegiances change over time, tribal leaders actively patrolled the boundaries of identity and erected sharp divisions to demarcate "us" versus "them." They used a sacred line between cosmos (our world) and chaos (disorder) to set the boundaries of identity. Often, the only way for a people to protect their cosmos is to destroy any real or imagined "evil other." Moral order is maintained. We see this in the sacred histories that circulated. It is not enough to escape from slavery in Egypt; Yahweh has to drown Pharaoh and his army. It is not enough for God to establish ritual laws for the Hebrews; God has to kill off an entire generation that lived in Egypt before the people can enter the promised land. Cultural purity became a prerequisite for God's blessing.

This fear of the other also had implications for daily life. Community leaders encouraged intratribal marriage to keep people from marrying outside of the group. Ethnic difference was emphasized and exaggerated to promote belief in the distinctiveness of a people. And matters of difference were embellished to underscore the point that neighbors were enemies who played on a different team. This is why stories about the total defeat of one's enemy were as common in the ancient Near East as headlines like "Packers Crush the Bears" are on ESPN.com today.

Should we be sickened by the genocidal language in Deuteronomy? Absolutely. Should we be surprised by it? Absolutely not. People in the ancient world were no more tribal than many of us in modern society today. Consider political chants to "build a wall" to keep out immigrants or executive orders that attempt to ban entrance to the United States for people living in seven predominantly Muslim countries. Less than policy prescriptions, these are mostly rhetorical methods to establish an in-group identity among specifically targeted white Americans. Both xenophobia and in-group bias remain a central feature of modern life.

A cursory glance at the contours of modernity reveals that the roots of race-based slavery and racial injustice in the Americas carry the lasting marks of these indefensible biblical myths. With regard to the institution of slavery in the United States, few stories were referenced as often as the cursing of Ham in Genesis 9. As slavery became increasingly associated with people of African descent in the seventeenth century, defenders of slavery yanked the curse of Ham from the pages of Scripture and applied it to their context. The myth became both a lens and a mirror through which white male property owners could view their world and themselves. This lens was especially strong in the antebellum South due to the high place of honor in that society.

On the one hand, the values of Christianity and protection of the household shaped southern society insofar as many regarded characters like Noah, Abraham, and Lot as strong examples of southern white manhood. On the other hand, since advocates of slavery went out of their way to depict Africans as lacking in self-control, sexually deviant, and deficient in mental capacity, they could advance the argument that Africans were born into servitude. Like Ham, Africans were apparently cursed, fated to live under the authority of other races. Many southern white men saw it as their moral obligation to keep Africans enslaved to maintain law and order in the United States.

The writings of Josiah Priest provide a clear example. His *Bible Defence of Slavery and the Origin, History, and Fortunes of the Negro Race* (1851) traces racial differences on the planet back to Noah. According to Priest, God caused Japheth "to be born white, while HE caused Ham to be born black." On the temperament of black people, Priest speaks of

> violence of temper, exceedingly beastly lusts, and lasciviousness in its worst feature, going beyond the force of the passions as possessed in common by the other races of men. Second, the word signifies deceit, dishonesty, treachery, lowmindedness, and malice. . . . What a group of horrors are here couched in the word Ham, all agreeing, in the most surprising manner, with the color of Ham's skin, as well as his real character as a man, during his own life, as well as with that of his race, even now.

Priest equates the name Ham with blackness and associates negative character traits with black skin. He thereby concludes that since the reestablishment of humanity after the flood, people of dark skin were condemned by God to serve the lighter races, just as Ham was sentenced to serve Japheth. According to this line of reasoning, the history of European conquest and the North Atlantic slave trade all begins with Noah passing out sloppy drunk.

Priest also traces variations of color and hair texture among people of color back to divine design. For Priest, color variation in the antebellum South had nothing to do with the prevalent practice of white male slaveholders maintaining mixed-race families with enslaved black women. Priest contends that the differences between light and dark skin and "straight" versus "woolly" hair connect to mental capacity. As was common in the nineteenth century, he claimed that "the straight-haired Negro has ever been found to be more intellectual, enterprising, and comely to look upon than the other race, who, from the earliest of times have been made of slaves."

This conception of race based on Genesis 9:20–27 reached beyond the borders of the United States and the antebellum South. "Scientific" racists and members of the Dutch Reformed Church in South Africa promoted the belief that "Bantus"—a general label for over five hundred different ethnic groups in Central and South Africa—were descendants of Ham. Theologians and politicians appealed to this crude racial distinction to justify apartheid laws in the twentieth century, including the Bantu Education Act of 1953 that legalized not only racial segregation but also directed black children toward positions of nonskilled labor.

German and Belgian colonizers appealed to this same logic in the Great Lakes region of East Africa at the turn of the twentieth century. White European race theorists labeled the Tutsis in Rwanda, with their supposed resemblance to Europeans due to their lighter skin color, as a lost race of Christians of Ethiopian descent. The Hutus, on the other hand, were labeled children of Ham as a result of their darker hue. Tutsis were provided with greater levels of access to power, and Catholic schools, which dominated the colonial education system, openly discriminated against the Hutus. Invariably this led to a two-tier track of employment, as Tutsis enjoyed administrative and political jobs while the Hutus were forced into manual labor, often as plantation workers.

This sort of tribal division based on phenotype, which was arbitrary at best, sowed the seeds of resentment for decades. When the monarchy dissolved and Belgian troops withdrew from Rwanda in 1962, a power vacuum emerged. Consequently, a quarter of a million people died as a result of armed conflicts over the next few decades, culminating in the 1993 genocide of Tutsis by the Hutu majority. Even here the Hamitic myth oversaw the murderous blades of Hutu soldiers butchering Tutsi families en masse. When Hutu leader Léon Mugesera called on all Hutus to send the Tutsis back to Ethiopia, there was no mistaking what he meant. The German and Belgian imperialists were long gone, but the myth of Ham that they introduced to divide the country remained in the cultural air.

## Carrying the Weight of Sexual Violence

The second narrative for us to analyze involves Abraham's nephew Lot and Lot's daughters. This is a mind-boggling tale of power, violence, and abuse. It begins with the arrival of two angels to the city of Sodom. Lot is not aware of their heavenly identity, yet as an act of hospitality, he repeatedly pleads with them to stay at his house. He organizes a feast for them, after which he prepares to retire for the evening. Chaos soon erupts:

> But before they lay down, the men of the city, the men of Sodom, both young and old, all the people to the last man, surrounded the house; and they called to Lot, "Where are the men who came to you tonight? Bring them out to us, so that we may know them." Lot went out of the door to the men, shut the door after him, and said, "I beg you, my brothers, do not act so wickedly. Look, I have two daughters who have not known a man; let me bring them out to you, and do to them as you please; only do nothing to these men, for they have come under the shelter of my roof. (Gen. 19:4–8)

The writer captures humanity at its worst. Sodom represents an utterly depraved people. Most biblical commentators agree that the overarching aim of this text is to demonstrate Lot's pious attempts at hospitality. By extending this level of grace toward the visitors, Lot strikes an extreme contrast against the otherwise inhospitable people of Sodom. For this reason, one might argue that the primary protagonist of this story is not Lot but Lot's uncle Abraham. Why? The answer is in the previous chapter.

Genesis 18 offers Abraham, the father of the faith, as an exemplar of hospitality and righteousness. It begins with Abraham receiving angelic visitors. It is evident that the Lot story mirrors the language and description of the Abraham story. Whereas Lot was sitting at the entrance of the city, Abraham is sitting at the entrance of his tent. When Abraham sees the visitors, he runs toward them and bows down to the ground, similar to Lot's reaction in Genesis 19. Abraham pleads with the visitors to stay, and he prepares a feast for them. Abraham is a noble man of honor who demonstrates to the visitors that he has what my mother used to call "good home training." Abraham models radical hospitality and righteousness and is thereby lifted up as an honorable model of excellence for his nephew Lot to emulate in his own household.

After this scene, Genesis 18:16–33 presents Abraham as a public defender negotiating a plea agreement with God on behalf of the city of Sodom. Abraham is obviously concerned about the city because of Lot and his family. Abraham also appears to be testing the fidelity of God to the righteous. No matter how wicked the crowd, God will not forsake those who live faithful and honorable lives. This sets up the scene in the next chapter where the storyline is not just about the wickedness of the city that merits destruction, but the promises of God to protect the virtuous.

The wickedness of Sodom is complete. The author reveals that all men of the city, "both young and old, all the people to the last man," show up at Lot's door. Lot's lone attempt at hospitality is useless against such a ravenous culture of inhospitality. Whereas Lot sought to host, the townsmen sought to harm; insofar as Lot represents honor, the townsmen represent abuse. Nothing can appease their passions. They demand for Lot to open the door and bring out the visitors so that they may "know them," which is a euphemism for sexual encounter. This is where the text gets particularly problematic, as it seems that the author is willing to have Lot meet the crowd's demented extreme with his own unthinkable offer. The Bible is silent on what Lot was feeling at this moment, which makes the picture that much more disturbing. To defend the honor of his house and protect his guests, Lot resorts to the desperate act of offering his virgin daughters to the gang to be raped. Are we to believe that the safety of any male guest and the honor of any male host is more important than protecting one's own daughters? It sure seems so.

And what about Lot's daughters? Put on the lenses of love and look their way. We cannot ignore what Lot's daughters may have been feeling at this point. They have no voice. They have no say. Yet they are listening through the door as their father offers them up as a sexual "peace offering" to pacify the crowd. Lot deems his daughters as less valuable than the male visitors. Lot gives up their bodies for male consumption with little regard for his daughters' desires, wants, or feelings. I tremble at the thought of what it must feel like to be so vulnerable and powerless. Unfortunately, this is the experience of so many who have endured the horror of sexual violence. There is often a double injustice, as victims, particularly young women like Lot's daughters, are twice victimized: they are victims of their assailant and of a larger culture that often pressures them into silence (not to mention the added pain of experiencing such violence at the hands of a parent). As one who serves at a major university, I find these interrelated problems of assault and silencing to be particularly acute. The prevalence of sexual assault on college campuses and universities is made more deplorable by campus cultures where victims do not feel protected.

Recently the Association of American Universities (AAU) released data from a sexual conduct survey in which students from twenty-seven universities, including Harvard, participated. Among the more than 60 percent of Harvard College female seniors who responded to the survey, about one-third report having experienced some form of "nonconsensual sexual contact" since entering college. Moreover, half of those women who experienced nonconsensual contact reported it as experienced or attempted penetration. In spite of these statistics, few sexual assaults on campus are reported to the authorities. Depending on the type of behavior, only between 5 to 28 percent of victims reported their assault to campus officials or law enforcement officers. The apparent variance between those who reported sexual assault in the survey and those who felt comfortable coming forward to report their attack to campus officials is telling. Somehow our campuses have sent the message that victims of sexual assault do not have a voice. In some ways, we have told victims that we do not take their pain seriously.

Fortunately, there are some courageous women in our society who will not be silenced. Emma Sulkowicz, a visual arts major, turned the pain of her experience into performance art in order to make a point to campus administrators at Columbia University in New York City. She took to *Time* magazine to describe her account of rape at the outset of her sophomore year and what she alleges was the university's mishandling of her case. Despite two other students who alleged that the same male classmate assaulted them as well, the man was not expelled from the university. Thus, Sulkowicz took to toting around her mattress everywhere she went on campus as a symbol of her burden. She titled her performance, which she turned into her senior thesis, "Carry That Weight." From August to when she walked across the stage at Senior Class Day in May, Sulkowicz carried the mattress. Her thesis soon became a rallying cry for campus activists across the country. Student protestors even created "Carry That Weight Together," a National Day of Action to stand in solidarity with all victims of sexual abuse. Whether Lot's daughters, young women on our campuses, or women in our churches, too many carry the weight of abuse alone and in silence.

There is one final point I wish to make about this story of Lot and his daughters. The reason I have underscored its emphasis on hospitality is due to modern associations of Sodom with homosexuality. Beginning in the eleventh century CE, interpretations of this story reflected the sexual obsessions of the Catholic Church in the Middle Ages. Such a view ignores that, historically, gang rape was the means by which warring nations shamed defeated opponents, a sordid expression of violence and hatred. This continues throughout our world today. So to equate such sexual violence with either heterosexual or homosexual activity is to miss the point of the narrative altogether. The story of Sodom in Genesis 19 is about inhospitality and sexual violence. To argue that this story is a condemnation of same-sex desire is to underscore the unthinkable point that Lot's offering up his daughters to the male crowd for a "hetero" gang rape is more acceptable.

This text makes clear that in the mind of the author, control over the lives of girls is completely a male prerogative. To proffer the rape of girls in order to illustrate the extreme measures Lot was willing to take to defend his honor and be hospitable to male guests should leave all of us sick to our stomachs. There is no defense. Nor is any apology sufficient. At some point, as people of faith, we just have to be willing to say that on some matters the biblical writers were wrong. Period. Some illustrations and metaphors, even if culturally acceptable in their world, are deplorable and wrong in our world.

### Texts of Terror

To underscore the point that some illustrations and metaphors in the Bible are always inappropriate, let's conclude this chapter with a few more examples. Biblical scholar Phyllis

Trible famously discusses them in her book *Texts of Terror.*
For instance, the writings of the Hebrew prophets are saturated with sexual and violent imagery to represent God's commitment to an otherwise obstinate nation. In Ezekiel 16, the
writer likens Jerusalem to a little girl born of an Amorite father
and a Hittite mother (both avowed enemies of Jerusalem).
The mother abandoned the baby in the blood of her birth in
the land of the Canaanites. God took pity on her, cleaned her,
raised her, and when her "breasts were formed," God adorned
her in beautiful leather, linen, and expensive jewels. But the
girl became obsessed with her beauty and the attention it com-
manded. She became a harlot and began giving herself to other
nations, not out of need, but to satisfy her lustful desires.

Ezekiel 16 describes God as a committed husband—a husband who demonstrates his love by exploding in wrath:

> I will gather all your lovers, with whom you took pleasure, all
> those you loved and all those you hated; I will gather them
> against you from all around, and will uncover your naked-
> ness to them, so that they may see all your nakedness. I will
> judge you as women who commit adultery and shed blood
> are judged, and bring blood upon you in wrath and jealousy.
> I will deliver you into their hands, and they shall throw down
> your platform and break down your lofty places; they shall
> strip you of your clothes and take your beautiful objects and
> leave you naked and bare. They shall bring up a mob against
> you, and they will stone you and cut you to pieces with their
> swords. They shall burn your houses and execute judgments
> on you in the sight of many women; I will stop you from
> playing the whore, and you shall also make no more pay-
> ments. So I will satisfy my fury on you, and my jealousy shall
> turn away from you; I will be calm, and will be angry no
> longer. (Ezek. 16:37–42)

According to this image, God's key attributes are male dominance, power, and control. In multiple ways, this passage
reinforces an understanding of the female body as primarily

an object for male protection and domination. The narrative advances the belief that love and care come with the price of submission, obedience, and abuse.

The pronouncement also elucidates a relationship between male dominance and sexual violence. Few health professionals regard rape as primarily about passionate desire but instead about power and control. A rapist seizes control over the life of the victim. Rape is thus a declaration of war against another's body with the sole purpose being to conquer and subdue. It is a dangerous and egregious error for anyone to employ a marital metaphor that depicts God as a jealous husband filled with rage. As Scripture, such a scene religiously authorizes the public humiliation and mutilation of any female body that dishonors masculine power. Nothing can or should justify this type of behavior.

Another dimension of domestic violence involves the emotional roller coaster from rage to reconciliation that characterizes many abusive relationships. Recall a common image of the abusive partner, who shifts from inflicting physical harm to showering his spouse with expensive gifts and flowers. There is a paradoxical message here that to express love one must first show violence. Love is always bound with pain. We see such an example in the second chapter of Hosea. Hosea is the eighth-century BCE prophet known for his harsh moral pronouncements against the nation of Israel. We find one of the earliest written examples of the marriage metaphor between God and the nation in the book of Hosea. The metaphor takes the form of Hosea's biography, as God commands the prophet to marry a woman of ill-repute named Gomer. The couple has a son and a daughter together, and a third child is born under questionable circumstances.

This marriage symbolizes God's covenant relationship with Israel. The entire second chapter provides a narrative of how Hosea will deal with Gomer. He declares that Gomer (Israel) will pursue all of her lovers to no avail and then realize that it was Hosea (God) who purchased her grain, wine, oil, and lavish silver and gold. Hosea then describes how he will "uncover her shame in the sight of her lovers, and no one shall rescue her out of my hand" (2:10). And after he strips away all of her possessions, he shifts his position from violent rage to seductive persuasion: "I will now allure her, and bring her into the wilderness, and speak tenderly to her" (v. 14). So just as God's rage is woven into the fabric of God's love and devotion, so is rage woven into the husband's love for his wife.

One has to wonder whether biblical writers were projecting the insecurities of patriarchs in the ancient Near East who feared losing control of their household and thus their social honor. This sort of vulnerability might help to explain, though not excuse, the prevalence of the marriage metaphor in the Hebrew Bible in which God is a dishonored husband trying to maintain his obligation to Israel, a sexually lascivious wife. Fear of losing control of one's wife and status in the community animated intense jealousy. Anything ancient men felt so strongly, surely God must feel the same way about a "whoring" nation. Thus, with this metaphorical point of identification, God legitimates a violent form of love and punishment that can only be considered abusive.

Unfortunately, these particular texts degrade human personality, as there is nothing life affirming about such metaphors for God. Of course, there are others throughout the Bible. They were influenced by the unjust dimensions of their context and do not merit being the last words of God. We have witnessed the damaging impact on the faith when biblical interpreters use the Bible to justify slavery and genocide, or turn a blind eye toward rape, domestic violence, and child abuse. There is no reason for us to ignore or excuse the immorality of these writings any longer.

**For Further Reference**

Garcia, Hector. *Alpha God: The Psychology of Religious Violence and Oppression.* Amherst, NY: Prometheus Books, 2015.
Gourevitch, Philip. *We Wish to Inform You That Tomorrow We Will Be Killed with Our Families.* New York: Farrar, Straus & Giroux, 1999.

Hill Fletcher, Jeannine. *The Sin of White Supremacy*. Maryknoll, NY: Orbis Books, 2017.

Johnson, Sylvester A. *The Myth of Ham in Nineteenth-Century American Christianity: Race, Heathens, and the People of God*. New York: Palgrave Macmillan, 2004.

Jordan, Mark. *The Invention of Sodomy in Christian Theology*. Chicago: University of Chicago Press, 1997.

Knust, Jennifer. *Unprotected Texts: The Bible's Surprising Contradictions about Sex and Desire*. San Francisco: HarperOne, 2011.

Trible, Phyllis. *Texts of Terror: Literary-Feminist Readings of Biblical Narratives*. Philadelphia: Fortress Press, 1984.

Weems, Renita. *Battered Love: Marriage, Sex, and Violence in the Hebrew Bible*. Minneapolis: Fortress Press, 1995.

# PART III

## The Practice of Subverting Authority

# 7

## Setting the Captives Free

## A Gospel Ethic

> The Jesus movement articulates a quite different under-
> standing of God because it had experienced in the praxis
> of Jesus a God who called not Israel's righteous and pious
> but its religiously deficient and its social underdogs.
> —Elisabeth Schüssler Fiorenza

> Either love is something other than emotion or the Great
> Commandment is useless.
> —Paul Tillich

### Laying Claim to Jesus

The late, great Gabriel García Márquez is one of my favorite
writers. The Colombian Nobel Prize winner is best known for
short stories and for prominent novels such as *One Hundred
Years of Solitude* and *Love in the Time of Cholera*. A particular reason that so many appreciate García Márquez's work is
his ability to capture both grim circumstances and transcen-
dent aspects of existence in his writing. The realms of the natural and supernatural are in constant conversation with one
another. The mundane and miraculous intersect with ease.

Literary scholars now refer to this style of storytelling as **magical realism**.

García Márquez's short story "The Handsomest Drowned Man in the World" exemplifies the style. The story tells of a fully intact corpse that washes ashore near a small coastal village. The author describes the villagers as diminutive, dull, and insipid. People no longer plant flowers or tend to their homes; residents rarely celebrate life or one another. Yet when residents of the village look upon the face and body of the corpse, they collectively come to view him as the strongest, largest, most handsome man they have ever seen. They name him Esteban. And they conclude that wherever Esteban lived, his house would have been the largest, his flowers the best kept, and his wife the happiest. When the men of the village discover that no man fitting Esteban's description is missing from neighboring villages, they all rejoice. "He's ours," they declare.

The people prepare a splendid funeral for Esteban, replete with flowers discovered elsewhere and clothes stitched from sails. As they carry his body to the cliff to cast it back into the sea, the villagers begin to notice the desolation of their streets, the colorlessness of their community, and the smallness of their own hopes and dreams. Esteban forever changes their village. They begin to plant flowers, paint their homes, and dream of a future, a future in which their carefully tended community will cause the captain of each passing ship to declare, "Look over there. That's Esteban's village."

This story contains a powerful moral lesson about admiration and transformation. The deceased man came to life in the latent hopes, dreams, and aspirations of the village. Their admiration for all that he stood for revived in them spiritual strivings and an appreciation for love and beauty. They now desired to be a people worthy of Esteban.

As a scholar of religion and a person of faith, I can connect this story to the writings about Jesus relatively easily. In a general sense, the four canonical Gospels—Matthew, Mark, Luke, and John—provide a unique style of writing that prefigures this genre of magical realism. The supernatural world often breaks into the mundane in the Gospels, and miracles are understood as very real options for healing and hope. The blind receive their sight. The deceased are resurrected. The chronically ill are made whole.

The Gospels are not a detailed history of Jesus' life. Less than a first-hand biographical account, they tell us more about what Jesus had become in the minds and hearts of those who joined the Jesus movement. Written roughly between 75 and 100 CE, the Gospels capture stories about Jesus that were circulating among his early followers who never actually met him but who nevertheless made him their own. Hence, the Gospels are more concerned with the public dimensions of Jesus' ministry than with any private dimensions of his life. Mark and John tell us nothing about Jesus' early days. Matthew and Luke provide (different) birth narratives, yet Matthew jumps quickly to Jesus' adult ministry. Luke offers a single story about Jesus' adolescence, which is clearly to prefigure his adult activity. The Gospels, then, are more akin to a spiritual biography that is concerned with identifying seemingly miraculous exemplary features of a leader's life.

The Gospels are similar to the genre of magical realism where the past and present are interwoven into a narrative form that disrupts linear chronology. Gospel narratives often recall and reflect past events recorded in the Hebrew Bible. Matthew, Mark, Luke, and John situate Jesus within the sacred history of Judaism in order to imbue his life with the authority of the biblical traditions. Think about how Herod's decree to kill the firstborn son mirrors Pharaoh's efforts in the book of Exodus (Matt. 2:13; Exod. 1:15–22). Jesus' power to calm the storm (Luke 8:23–25) as well as to feed thousands of people (Matt. 14:19) connects him to Moses and Moses's miraculous acts of provision for the people as they wandered in the wilderness (Exod. 16). And Jesus' ability to raise children from the dead and cure leprosy recall the Hebrew prophets Elijah (1 Kgs. 17:14) and Elisha (2 Kgs. 5:14).

Although Jesus was a historical figure, his life is detailed in the Gospels as sacred history. As historical evidence concerning the feats of King David in Israel or Abraham Lincoln in the United States have become the grist for subsequent generations to lionize their accomplishments into sacred myths, the same is true of Jesus. Something attracted many to him and caused them to embrace his message. So though I am not suggesting that Jesus was merely a figment of his followers' imaginations like Esteban was, I do believe that García Márquez's tale can provide us with insight into how members of the Jesus movement accepted Jesus as risen savior—even insight as to why millions, like myself, continue to embrace Jesus today.

## The Gospels

The Gospels are a collection of sacred stories that circulated among the earliest members of the Jesus movement. These stories about a wise and compassionate Christ (a Greek translation of the Hebrew word for Messiah, "anointed") speak to the spiritual and material needs of everyday people. Accounts of Jesus' teachings provide spiritual visions of how followers might reimagine themselves and their place in the larger world. Through Jesus, people saw an otherworldly kingdom free of violence, illness, and sorrow. Religious hierarchies are flattened. Ethnic barriers are diminished. And God's love can redeem anyone from a Roman centurion to a Jewish tax collector. Whether wealthy or poor, all had a place in Jesus' message. This helps to explain how people from across multiple sectors of society found a message of hope, healing, and faith in Jesus. These early communities embraced a radical experiment to live lives that were worthy of Jesus, their Lord and Savior.

Another dimension to the Gospels is its social critique about power, privilege, and empire. For example, miracle accounts open up new possibilities about who is welcome and worthy in the kingdom of God. A leper, a bleeding woman, the blind, and the demon-possessed (that is, the mentally ill) would have all ranked quite low according to the prevailing practices of purity politics within Judaism at this time. Yet they were all beloved and embraced by Jesus. Disaffected peasants and the socially despised found in Jesus a savior who viewed them as blessed children of God.

This style of spiritual biography, however, can present interpretive difficulties. Some of this has to do with illustrations and allusions that spoke to audiences that are far removed from our experience today. References to barren fig trees and camels passing through the eyes of needles can easily confuse the modern reader. It is also easy to become consumed with attempts to defend the supernatural accuracy of miracle accounts; we lose sight of what the story might be trying to reveal about Jesus. Therefore, let's put on the lenses of love in order to undertake the interpretive process.

Recall that one of the early steps of the interpretive process begins with establishing the social and historical context. We want to attend to the questions of who, when, where, and what. Of course, the primary protagonist of the Gospels is Jesus. We saw earlier that the Gospels were not written by those who were direct witnesses of the events reported. Writing anonymously was standard practice among scribal cultures in the ancient Near East, as documents were produced more by social institutions or groups oriented around schools of thought than by individual writers. Christian communities didn't even assign names to these Gospels until the second century CE.

Because the authors are unknown, we will focus on what the Gospels might have conveyed to early followers who embraced a risen Jesus as their own. Each Gospel provides a powerful example of how communities imagined Jesus as a model of divinity who stood in stark ethical contrast to the prevailing gods of Rome. In a world that commonly associated the sacred with social status and gods with political power, such as the pharaohs of Egypt and emperors of Rome, Jesus became a counterdeity. Those in the region with diminished honor, little status, and even less power—which included everyone from wealthy widows to the poor and destitute—embraced a messiah who embodied the teachings of the Hebrew prophets. Jesus was the ruler of a different kind of kingdom.

Matthew, Mark, and Luke are the first three Gospels in the New Testament. Known as the **Synoptic Gospels**, they are distinct narratives with a common theme that share a similar storyline, miracle accounts, and emphasis on the kingdom of God. The writers of Matthew and Luke used Mark as their original guide. So even though Matthew is listed first in the New Testament, Mark is believed to be the oldest Gospel and what created the mold for Matthew and Luke.

In the late first century, those reading Mark would have noticed a not so subtle challenge of the Roman Empire from the outset. The Gospel appropriates the language of Roman officials to describe the *euangelion*, or good news, of Jesus Christ (1:1). Mark was written around the time of the Jewish war of revolt against the Roman Empire (66–73 CE). Hostilities increased between Jewish Palestine and Rome in the three decades following Jesus' crucifixion. Rome selected particularly harsh governors for the region who often sought to introduce Roman religious symbols in Jerusalem in general and in the temple in particular. Around 40 CE, the Roman emperor Caligula attempted to place a statue of his own depiction in the temple. Such efforts led to civil unrest and violent protests by revolutionary Jews who refused to stand by idly and witness their homeland desecrated. Jewish rebellion led to Roman reprisals. Following a three-year standoff between rebels and Rome, the empire unleashed a mass assault on Judea. The Romans seized the city of Jerusalem, executed over five thousand Judeans, and utterly destroyed the temple.

The Gospel of Mark captures these events with prophetic and apocalyptic language. Mark 13 depicts the horrors of the period most graphically. In predicting the destruction of the temple, Jesus asks his disciples, "Do you see these great buildings? Not one stone will be left here upon another; all will be thrown down" (v. 2). Jesus then encourages his disciples to remain calm when they hear of "wars and rumors of wars" and when "nation will rise against nation, and kingdom against kingdom." He offers these developments as "the birth pangs" that will usher in a new age (v. 8). After telling them that they will be brought to trial, persecuted, and even betrayed and hated by family members for their commitment to him, Jesus encourages his disciples to take comfort. Just when it appears darkest, "they will see the 'Son of Man coming in clouds' with great power and glory. Then he will send out the angels, and gather his elect from the four winds, from the ends of the earth to the ends of heaven" (vv. 26–27).

The readers and hearers of Mark's Gospel would have seen themselves and their situation in this chapter. The world seemed to be coming to an end for Jews in Jerusalem. Hence, the Gospel seeks to convey an important message to members of the Jesus movement. Despite the extreme physical violence and their severe emotional suffering, in Christ, victory and defeat, success and failure, and winners and losers are not always as they appear. The good news does not belong to Caesar but rather to Jesus and those who follow him. It is not the seemingly powerful and mighty, "but the one who endures to the end [who] will be saved" (v. 13). Simply put, salvation comes to those who go the way of the cross of Christ, not the Roman crown. For Jews living under the ominous clouds of bloodshed and brutality, this was indeed good news.

The case is similar in Matthew's Gospel. It, too, depicts the teachings of Jesus as subversive to conventional power and authority. More than Mark, and in contrast to Luke, Matthew's constant allusions to the Hebrew Bible let the community know that the God of Israel will not be compromised by the Jewish elite who seem more interested in maintaining power than adhering to the Hebrew tradition. To the contrary, Jesus is the true expression of the God who delivered their people out of Egypt. Jesus is the new Moses whom God raises up for the cause of liberation for his people (Exod. 1:8–2:10; 3:1–10; Matt. 2:13–23). His teachings and miracles in Matthew harken to Hebrew prophets such as Elijah and Elisha, who often showed compassion for the poor, widows, and the diseased (1 Kgs. 17:10–24; 2 Kgs. 4:2–7; 5:1–19).

A key feature of Matthew is the Beatitudes, Jesus' list of blessings, which include:

> Blessed are the poor in spirit,
> for theirs is the kingdom of heaven.
> Blessed are those who mourn,
> for they will be comforted.
> Blessed are the meek,
> for they will inherit the earth.
> Blessed are those who hunger and thirst for righteousness,
> for they will be filled.
> Blessed are the merciful,
> for they will receive mercy. (5:3–7)

Such teachings in Matthew echo Mark's message of social inversion. It's not the powerful and mighty who are the victors. In God's kingdom, the social underdogs and the outcasts can claim the victory. The poor, those who mourn, the merciful, the peacemakers, and those persecuted for righteousness are the real winners. For wherever you find them, you will find God (Matt. 25:31–45).

The writer of Luke cast his net broader than the writers of Mark and Matthew, but he makes similar points about Jesus. Luke's Gospel was written for a wider audience than the other two Synoptics. Its language and metaphors are more general and thus accessible to a larger Greco-Roman audience. Its illustrations and parables would have resonated with those who may not have been as well versed in the Torah yet still found the teachings of the Jewish tradition instructive and compelling.

In Luke, Jesus' birth narrative uses language from the Roman Empire to announce Jesus' ministry. The Mediterranean world regarded and referred to Caesar as the *soter* ("savior") of the world. This was based on Rome's claim that Caesar alone brought peace and stability throughout the provinces. So when the Gospel places "good news of great joy for all the people" in the mouth of an angel of the Lord, the writer is undercutting the authority of the empire (Luke 2:10). The Gospel then uses the term *soter,* normally reserved for Caesar, and applies it to Jesus: "To you is born this day in the city of David a Savior, who is the Messiah, the Lord" (v. 11). The narrative proceeds to make its case over the next twenty-two chapters. Jesus offers an alternative and more secure path of salvation. Jesus is the true savior.

Nowhere does Luke strike this theme of inversion more clearly than in the parables. Luke's Gospel contains the largest number of these short metaphoric tales, including eighteen that are unique to Luke. In chapter 3, we discussed the parable of the Good Samaritan, but there are others that register the same tone of compassion. Parables such as the Wedding Feast, the Lost Sheep, the Lost Coin, and the Prodigal Son invert cultural conventions and typical social relations. In first-century Palestine, not unlike our world today, daily behaviors privileged the powerful, celebrated the popular, and bestowed honor upon those who appeared most successful. Luke's parables paint a contrasting picture of the kingdom of God. By doing so, these parables offer moral lessons about God's love for us. Invariably, then, they offer lessons about what the reception of God's love demands from us. It's not just about us and God. The parables are about us and our neighbors.

Finally, there is John's Gospel. This Gospel is different in content and character from the three Synoptic Gospels. The community that produced this book underscores an important point about the first-century Mediterranean world: it is difficult to draw sharp lines of division between ancient Judaism and Greek philosophical influence. John's Gospel reveals the particular influence of Jewish Wisdom literature and appeals to what the Greeks understood to be universal forms of knowledge. John is a very philosophical text. With fewer parables and aphorisms, John is full of long passages and complex narratives that attempt to explain the universality of Jesus' divine identity. The Gospel offers Jesus as the way, the truth, and the light for all humanity throughout time. John's Gospel thus locates Jesus in the beginning of creation. In John, Jesus is less human and more cosmic; he is less flesh and more spirit. Thus, the imagery of John places greater emphasis on the supernatural and accentuates the immaterial, as is evident in the Gospel's opening verses: "In the beginning was the Word, and the Word was with God, and the Word was God. He was in the beginning with God. All things came into being through him, and without him not one thing came into being. What has come into being in him was life, and the life was the light of all people" (John 1:1–4). Despite its philosophical content, John provides stories of the unbelievable to make a point about the ethical. Standing with the marginalized and embracing the stranger are the overarching themes that shape this fourth Gospel.

Let's look at Jesus' inaugural miracle in John, in which he turns water into wine at a wedding party in Cana (2:1–11). To comprehend the aim of the story is to know something about weddings in the ancient Mediterranean. Weddings were week-long celebrations. Since the peasant class constituted about 90 percent of the Palestinian region during the first century, wedding celebrations provided an important counterpunch to the constant, dull blows of poverty.

It is instructive, then, that the Gospel of John locates God, in the person of Jesus, at a wedding. The writer introduces Jesus' wonder-working power to the community by having Jesus provide an apparent luxury to a peasant community. The ruling classes and elites should not have a monopoly on festive celebrations of love. All are worthy to celebrate and embrace the small joys of life. Hence, Jesus did more than turn water to wine. Through him, God revealed what it means to stand alongside those who thirst. Jesus' act was not about bringing attention to himself. It was about bringing attention to those living in the shadows of society, casting a light on their human- ity and human strivings. All are worthy of God's provisions. As we see in other places throughout the Gospels, God's bountiful banquet table is open to all.

## A Message of Hope and Wholeness

Miracle accounts are a central feature of the Gospels. They provide both mystical visions and social commentary. Miracles depict how the celestial can interrupt the quotidian rhythms of life. They also illustrate an ethic that inverts power and sub- verts worldly authority. As a result, an important dimension of the miracle stories is how they troubled prevailing purity politics of Jesus' day. By purity politics, I am referring to the shifting views of purity within Judaism during the time of Jesus. It is a "politics" because how a society understands and/ or argues about what is "clean" and "dirty" shapes the soci- ety. In every culture, this is how we categorize people, create physical boundaries, and even establish a social pecking order. Our views of purity and defilement determine who and what belongs where. Often factors such as economic status, race, citizenship, and sexuality inform our judgments.

Particular understandings of purity held sway in Jesus' day. To be clear, there has never been a single, universal understanding of purity within Judaism. Yet two dominant understandings of purity informed ancient Judaism. The first involved defilement associated with common activities that no person could avoid. They are listed in Leviticus 11–15 and Numbers 19. Such acts include touching the carcass of a dead animal, childbirth, cer- tain skin diseases, or preparing a body for burial. Where these acts were considered unclean, they were not viewed as sinful. This is why each defiling activity came with its own cleansing rituals. According to this view, defilement was just a natural part of life, even as it was important to participate in a sacred ritual to return to a state of purity.

The second understanding of purity involves behaviors that opposed holiness. These types of defilements are found in the Holiness Code in Leviticus 17–26. They include idolatry, theft, violating sexual taboos, and other acts that ran counter to established community mores. Such actions were not regarded as inevitable; they were sinful offenses against God and others. Therefore, daily activities that defiled and behaviors that countered holiness were not one in the same.

The problem with purity politics in any society is the way that it renders the most vulnerable as easy scapegoats. Those without social status and cultural capital are often the first to be blamed for betraying established standards and decorum. Blame tends to roll downhill and to land at the feet of the already disinherited and disaffected. Purity politics, then, helps to legitimate, if not ignore, the morality of those living in the upper echelons of society. This may be why Jesus said that it is much easier for some to see the speck in the eyes of others, rather than the plank in their own eye (Matt. 7:3).

Think about HIV/AIDS in the United States. Not long ago, those infected with HIV were the modern-day lepers. Housing and workplace discrimination was common. And most regarded HIV/AIDS as an inevitable and shameful death sentence, the just deserts of a sinful lifestyle. Awareness campaigns and medical developments have helped to shift the public perception and the politics of how we view those infected and affected by HIV/AIDS. Basketball legend Magic Johnson not only has survived but has thrived since publicly acknowledging his HIV status. This is wonderful.

Unfortunately, a cloud of shame around the disease remains for others. The disease is now largely associated with black and brown people in poor communities and underdeveloped countries. Similarly, its associations with men who have sex with other men remains an obstacle to open dialogue within many Christian congregations. I have buried more than a few friends and church members over the years who have died of AIDS-related illnesses and whose families have refused to acknowledge this fact publicly, even if it could help educate others about at-risk behaviors, treatment options, or even how to care for an infected love one. Though perception has shifted, we still have a long way to go.

Another example of contemporary purity politics is our treatment of the homeless population. Too often we treat the homeless among us as deviant and defiled. For example, an Episcopal congregation in Davidson, North Carolina, purchased a bronze statue of Jesus depicted as a vagrant asleep on a park bench. The only clue that reveals Jesus's identity is the nail piercing on his feet that reach out from underneath a tattered blanket. According to the church's rector, he intended for the sculpture to remind the community that faith ought to express itself in an active concern for the marginalized. All in the community did not agree. Some felt that depicting Jesus in this manner was disrespectful. One neighbor wrote the local paper to say that the image "creeps him out" and ought to be removed. This man must have felt that the weathered and possibly soiled body of a homeless person should not sit so close to the perceived sterility and sanctity of a suburban sanctuary. Another neighbor mistook the statue for a real person and called the police. This is my point about purity politics. They shape our sense of human value; they determine who is fit to be where.

No society seems to be immune from purity politics. Every community, country, and religious tradition has its ways of establishing social hierarchies based on who or what is deemed appropriate. As recent history teaches us, periods of social insecurity and strife often drive political and religious leaders to circle the wagons around those considered pure while alienating those viewed as different. The Positive Christianity movement in Nazi Germany fused Christian teachings with Nazi ideals of racial purity. More recently, the so-called Nashville Statement drafted by the Evangelical Council on Biblical Manhood and Womanhood (CBMW) condemns those who believe that a family can be anything other than a heterosexual married couple adhering to traditional gender roles. And the forty-fifth president of the United States, Donald J. Trump, won the 2016 general election with the slogan "Make America Great Again," which many Democrats and Republicans alike considered anti-Mexican, anti-Islamic, and overwhelmingly nativistic. In other words, purity is a common obsession among those attempting to secure their power. Weak leaders tend to need strong scapegoats.

Ancient Palestine provides us with an example of this dynamic. There were many cultural pressures impinging on Judaism at the turn of the first millennium. There was a strict political and economic hierarchy resulting from imperialism in the region. Jews, for all intents and purposes, were colonized subjects. Local leaders who seemingly cooperated with Rome curried favor and resources for themselves. With imperialism also came a fear of cultural domination. **Hellenization** (the spread of Greek culture) was a source of extreme anxiety throughout the region for generations. For a people who prided themselves on distinctiveness due to their faith, Hellenization proved a formidable threat. Fear of cultural domination often causes religious leaders to circle the wagons around their communities. These communities erect high walls of division between "us" and "them" and hold their own community members to impossible standards of behavior. More often than not, the alienated and marginalized are marked as the symptomatic carriers of cultural decline. The poor, powerless, and perceived aliens become easily identifiable representatives of all that is wrong with the society.

It is with these prevailing purity politics in mind that I want us to consider the miracle accounts. Each of the Synoptic Gospels records Jesus healing those with "leprosy," those who were "demon-possessed," and a woman with an "issue of blood." These conditions extended well beyond a mere physical illness in need of a cure. The actual diseases had far-reaching social implications with regard to who was fit to be where.

Consider the array of skin conditions that could fall under

the category of leprosy in the ancient world. Leviticus 13:45–46 prescribes a regimen for these patients: "The person who has the leprous disease shall wear torn clothes and let the hair of his head be disheveled; and he shall cover his upper lip and cry out, 'Unclean, unclean.' He shall remain unclean as long as he has the disease; he is unclean. He shall live alone; his dwelling shall be outside of the camp." Here we see that socially marking someone as defiled was more important than spiritual care for the afflicted. Religiosity trumps human relations. Shame outweighs compassion.

The purity politics associated with diseases such as leprosy also demonstrates that illness was more than an individual matter. Disease impacted a person's standing within the community, and even that person's relationship to the Divine. Individuals were marked spiritually, mentally, and physically as abnormal and impure. Illness thus ruptured relationships and created social alienation. The demon-possessed in the Gospels offer an instructive example. The demon-possessed man in Mark's account came from the tombs (Mark 5:1–20). He lived in social exile among the dead, as if he were a walking corpse. We can read Matthew's account of two demon-possessed men similarly (Matt. 8:28–34), as well as Luke's story of the Gerasene man (Luke 8:26–39). In each of these distinct accounts, the men mutilate themselves and cannot be contained by chains. The only place suitable for their defiled spirits was a herd of pigs, among the most defiled of unclean animals.

Finally, there is the woman with the issue of blood. This is a particularly beautiful miracle account because, as at other places in the Gospels, Jesus privileges the pain of a female character. We should not ignore the gendered dimension of ancient purity politics. Bloodshed associated with menstruation or childbirth rendered women unclean. This is why Mark's emphasis on the duration of her illness—twelve years—underscores the degree of her social exclusion (Mark 5:21–43). Simply being out in the crowd attempting to touch Jesus defied social convention (Lev. 15:25, 27). Yet she, like so many other characters who appear in the Gospels, was convinced that Jesus could offer the healing she needed.

Growing up in church, I remember numerous sermons on the woman with the issue of blood. Since the King James Version of the Bible was most common in the Methodist and Baptist churches of my youth, I always heard the woman's thoughts as "If I may touch but his clothes, I shall be whole." Couple this with the fact that we often sang the Andraé Crouch hymn, "Oh, It Is Jesus," whose chorus went

> Oh, it is Jesus
> Oh, it is Jesus
> It's Jesus in my soul.
> For I have touched the hem of His garment
> and His blood has made me whole.

Though I was smart enough as a kid to figure out that being "made whole" was about healing, I still found the phrase somewhat odd. Today I think differently. In fact, I prefer the notion of being made whole over healing. The concept of wholeness better captures the complexity of the social and spiritual imaginaries that these miracle accounts capture. For followers of Jesus, miracles are about so much more than removing a skin condition, mental illness, or hemorrhage. On the one hand, Jesus' miracles disrupt what had become an unfortunate yet normalized way of life for those who fell short of the established standard of health, happiness, and holiness. On the other hand, miracles serve as moral encouragement for someone whose back is against the proverbial wall. The miracles themselves heal.

The Gospels, then, portray a Jesus who provides the sort of healing that is concerned with more than curing a physical malady. Jesus provides a comprehensive recovery that includes curing disease, overcoming social marginalization, and eradicating spiritual estrangement. Like the miracle accounts featuring the Hebrew prophets, such as Elijah providing food to a widow and healing her son (1 Kgs. 17:10–16), Jesus' miracles speak to the personal, social, and spiritual impact that disease can have on any person, particularly those living in a culture of harsh purity politics. Jesus speaks to the disease and to the unjust social dynamics that rendered the person sick in body, mind, and spirit.

The Gospel miracle accounts also function similarly to the beatitudes and parables. They flip the prevailing cultural script. Whereas the politics of purity sought to contain and ostracize, Jesus' miracles offered the type of healing that includes and embraces. Whereas ancient purity politics labeled victims of disease as morally and spiritually deficient, we read that Jesus' love makes them as good and worthy of God's love as anyone else. Thus, Jesus does more than heal the characters in the miracle accounts. He reconnects people to their community and locates them in God's kingdom. Jesus heals. He also makes people whole.

## An Ethic of Compassion

The previous section demonstrated a way of reading the Gospels in general, and Jesus' miracles in particular. By channeling the Hebrew prophets, Jesus inverted the prevailing purity politics of first-century Judaism. The beatitudes, parables, and miracle accounts provided members of the Jesus movement a different narrative about their lives and God's love. Whereas extreme poverty, disease, and mental illness placed many on the margins of society and subjected them to being labeled as defiled and/or deviant, the Gospels present a Jesus who reminds these very people that they are precious in God's sight.

Biblical scholar Marcus Borg spent much of his illustrious career arguing that Jesus countered the prevailing politics of purity with a politics of compassion. For Borg, this was not an anti-Semitic framework of **supersessionism**; Jesus was not inaugurating a new movement based on compassion to counter the teachings of the Hebrew Bible, and his followers were not creating something new within Judaism. Jesus' emphasis on compassion was a rearticulation of God's character, a central concept of the Hebrew Bible. In fact, I would argue that compassion is a fundamental attribute to how ancient Israelites understood their God. It is a recurring theme beginning in the Law and extending through the Prophets and the Wisdom literature. When the infant nation encountered God at Mount Sinai, it was God who declared, "The Lord, the Lord, a God merciful and gracious, slow to anger, and abounding in steadfast love and faithfulness, keeping steadfast love for the thousandth generation, forgiving iniquity and transgression and sin" (Exod. 34:6–7). Israel's sacred history is quite clear. When the people were at their moral worst at Mount Sinai, God was at his merciful best.

One need look no further than the Psalms to read how central the theme of God's mercy is in the Hebrew tradition. God is presented as one who "established equity" in order to execute justice and righteousness (99:4). God answers the prayers of the destitute and will "hear the groans of the prisoners, to set free those who were doomed to die" (102:17, 20). And both Psalms 105 and 106 are songs of exaltation for a God who continued to extend steadfast love not because of, but in spite of the nation's merits. The Psalms make clear that in the Hebrew tradition, the name of God is compassion and mercy.

What is more, the example of compassion as a divine attribute is intended to inspire us to act compassionately. Numerous proverbs stress the importance of compassion as a social ethic. The tradition teaches that those who show compassion shall find favor in the sight of God and humanity (Prov. 3:3–4). Showing pity toward the poor is likened to lending unto God (19:17), and rejoicing in the downfall of one's enemy contradicts God's spirit of compassion for all who hurt (24:17–18). The absolute clearest expression of this social ethic is found in the book of Micah. The prophet makes a declaration in the form of a rhetorical question: "He has told you, O mortal, what is good; and what does the Lord require of you but to do justice, and to love kindness [compassion], and to walk humbly with your God?" (Mic. 6:8).

There are many examples in the Gospels of Jesus modeling this ethic of compassion. One of my personal favorites is found in John 4, the story of the woman at the well. Let's review our steps. First, identify the genre. Since it is one of the teachings of Jesus, we can read the narrative in isolation, even as we are aware of the larger themes associated with Jesus' miracles. Next, consult secondary sources such as *The New Interpreter's Bible*. When it comes to the Gospel of John, I am particularly fond of the writings of Gail O'Day and Susan Hylen. These resources help us to better understand the theological themes and sociohistorical context of the exchange. Finally, try to place yourself in the text with your lenses of love and compassion. What do you see? How do you feel?

First, the writer does not provide many details about the main character. We do not know her name. Nor do we know details regarding her background. We just know that she was a Samaritan, and, as noted previously, Jews in Judea and Galilee viewed Samaritans with contempt. Hence, this woman is far from a conventional ministry candidate. She realizes as much and makes this point clear when Jesus greets her at the well and asks her for a drink. She asks Jesus, "How is it that you, a Jew, ask a drink of me, a woman of Samaria?" Despite the cultural differences, she is the biblical character to have the longest dialogue with Jesus in any of the four Gospels. In fact, in John's Gospel, she is the first disciple to spread Jesus' teachings and encourage converts to the Jesus movement.

Second, Jews and Samaritans shared much more in common than not. They both adhered to a strict monotheism, practiced male circumcision, and adhered to the Torah. But sometime during the fifth century BCE, during the Persian reign, Samaritans decided that the temple did not belong in Jerusalem but rather on Mount Gerizim in the city of Shechem, the original capital of the United Kingdom of Israel. This distinction was enough to cause the Jewish elite in Jerusalem to brand the

Samaritans as aberrant and deviant. Psychotherapists might refer to this dynamic in Freudian terms, a narcissism of minor differences. This is to say, when competing communities share adjoining territories and other attributes, they engage in constant battle as a means of emphasizing what they believe makes them unique. No matter how much Galileans and Judeans exaggerated their differences with Samaritans to preserve their sense of distinctiveness, at the end of the day, it is more accurate to think of Jews and Samaritans as interrelated rather than archenemies. The more we fail to see ourselves in the perceived other, the more likely we are to keep projecting our own evil thoughts and vain desires upon them.

This is why when I sit down in the text with lenses of love, I do not see this woman as intending to be rude or disrespectful to Jesus. One might suspect that her response is more a matter of surprise than sass. Why would Jesus, a Galilean, ask her for water? God only knows what kind of treatment this woman has grown accustomed to from Galilean men and women as they pass through town on their way to and from the capital city of Jerusalem in Judea. I imagine that she is well aware of the intentional and unintentional slights, derogatory remarks, and commonplace indignities directed toward her on a daily basis.

For instance, I can imagine a Galilean father telling his kids to be mindful of Samaritans on their journey through Samaria. Galilean women may have pulled their children closer when Samaritans drew near. Children may have stared curiously while asking, "Is she one of them, Daddy? A Samaritan?" Maybe the Samaritan woman learned to hang back from the well until Galileans finished collecting water. The clouds of stigma can darken the minds of oppressed people even in their own neighborhoods.

Maybe this is what the Samaritan woman expected when she saw Jesus smile at her. "Here comes another one. I am not good enough for him to marry, but I'm perfect for an afternoon of sexual fulfillment," she may have thought, while trying to conceal her shame and disgust. A culture of masculine privilege certainly fueled the "oldest profession in the world" in the area. Coupling this with the details provided about this woman's personal life and relationships with many different husbands has led many biblical interpreters to mark this woman as one of "ill repute." This explains why in many Christian communities, "the woman at the well" has become a euphemism for a modern-day sex worker.

None of this seems to matter to Jesus. Maybe Jesus realized that it was quite possible for this woman to have been trapped in what was known as a levirate marriage in the ancient world (Deut. 25:5–6). After the death of multiple spouses, she was not allowed to leave the family but was just passed down for marriage to the oldest living brother-in-law upon the death of each husband. This was quite possible. Such knowledge could be why Jesus restrained judgment and condemnation and unleashed grace and mercy.

Again, empathy is aided when we have a fuller understanding of how every person, particularly the most vulnerable among us, is forced to make ethical choices under conditions not necessarily of their own making. It's been said that we should not judge another until we walk a mile in their shoes. One can add that it's also important to know how a person ended up walking along a particular path in the first place. Social environments and experiences of the past matter.

Compassion, then, is an outgrowth of empathy. Yet it takes empathy a step forward. Empathy is to know and understand from another's perspective. Such understanding may be as basic as acknowledging that all humans have fundamental emotional needs: recognition, respect, love, and security. Thus, acts of compassion are when we put this knowledge and understanding into action.

John 4:1–29 is beautiful and instructive when it comes to a demonstration of compassion. Neither the Samaritan woman nor Jesus provides an explanation of the woman's circumstances. Those who told this story did not feel the need to explain away this woman's life. Unlike Luke's account of Jesus' dealings with Samaritans, the Gospel of John does not predicate just upon the virtuousness of the Samaritans. In the parable of the Good Samaritan, the Samaritan proves himself more honorable than either the priest or the Levite. Similarly, in Luke's account of Jesus healing ten lepers, the only person thoughtful enough to give Jesus thanks is the Samaritan. The narratives in Luke, then, imply that a Samaritan's capacity to be more noble than Galileans or Judeans is why they deserve compassion. The Gospel of John adds no moral clause. Jesus' treatment of the Samaritan women is not predicated on her goodness any more than her marginalization as a Samaritan is based on her sinfulness. How deviant or holy her personal lifestyle is, is of little consequence. Jesus only sees a woman in desperate need of respect and recognition. He sees an opportunity to extend compassion.

In sum, Jesus' actions in John 4 demonstrate two important features about compassion. First, compassion is most powerful and transformative when it is least expected. Jesus does not treat compassion as a commodity to be exchanged in response to a plea or request. He just extends it because he is in a position to do so. Second, though compassion does not seek anything in return, the very act provides its own reward. Jesus seems as concerned about who he should be in his treatment of the Samaritan woman as he is about what she might or might not deserve. To participate in her dehumanization would be to diminish a part of his own moral self. As Proverbs 11:17 states, "Those who are kind reward themselves, but the cruel do themselves harm." Thus, to greet and treat a fellow human with the grace and compassion of God is to reflect God's loving-kindness and grace toward us.

We have considered in this chapter the ways parables, miracles, and compassion accounts moved early followers of Jesus to act. Jesus' depictions of an otherworldly kingdom with an inverted social ethic captured the hearts and minds of a cross section of Judean and Greco-Roman society. Similar to the villagers in García Márquez's short story, these followers laid claim to Jesus. Millions across this planet continue to lay claim to this risen Savior as well. He is ours. Hence, it is our responsibility to comport ourselves accordingly. If only compassion could flow so freely from those who profess Christ that subsequent generations would look back and declare, "Look over there. That's Jesus' village."

## For Further Reading

Borg, Marcus. *Jesus: Uncovering the Life, Teachings, and Relevance of a Religious Revolutionary.* San Francisco: HarperOne, 2008.

Byrne, Brendan. *The Hospitality of God: A Reading of Luke's Gospel.* Collegeville, MN: Liturgical Press, 2015.

Crossley, James. *Why Christianity Happened: A Sociohistorical Account of Christian Origins (26–50 CE).* Louisville, KY: Westminster John Knox Press, 2006.

Ehrman, Bart D. *Jesus before the Gospels: How the Earliest Christians Remembered, Changed, and Invented Their Stories of the Savior.* San Francisco: HarperOne, 2016.

Gench, Frances Taylor. *Back to the Well: Women's Encounters with Jesus in the Gospels.* Louisville, KY: Westminster John Knox Press, 2004.

Klawans, Jonathan. *Impurity and Sin in Ancient Judaism.* New York: Oxford University Press, 2000.

O'Day, Gail, and Susan Hylen. *John.* Westminster Bible Companion. Louisville, KY: Westminster John Knox Press, 2006.

Rivera, Mayra. *Poetics of the Flesh.* Durham, NC: Duke University Press, 2015.

# 8

## Reading Someone Else's Mail

### The Pauline Epistles

> So also our beloved brother Paul wrote to you according to the wisdom given him, speaking of this as he does in all his letters. There are some things in them hard to understand, which the ignorant and unstable twist to their own destruction, as they do the other scriptures.
>
> —2 Pet. 3:15–16

> To imagine that first Jesus and then his followers were in conflict with "the Jews," a conflict with the sequential climaxes that occurred when "the Jews" killed Jesus and then certain of his followers, is, of course, to ignore the fact that Jesus and his first followers were themselves Jews.
>
> —James Carroll

#### A One-Sided Conversation

The apostle Paul is among the most vital figures in world history. The reasons are many. More of his writings constitute the Christian Bible than anyone else's. Paul surpasses Jesus' disciples as the principal figure in the book of Acts, and he is presented as the dominant force spreading the Jesus movement to those outside of Judaism. Thirteen letters in the New Testament are traditionally attributed to Paul. Whether it was his intention or not, it is difficult to deny that Paul's teachings helped to establish Christianity as a new world religion.

Despite Paul's popularity and authority in the early church (or maybe because of it), he has also served as a lightning rod of controversy for centuries. Church leaders, political figures, and demagogues have used Paul's letters to justify some of the most hateful ideologies, social injustices, and inhumane practices of modernity. The examples are tragically vast and violent. The pages of Paul's letters are filled with blood from the butcher's knife of perverse interpretations.

We can locate Christian anti-Judaism within the epistles of Paul. A particular reading of his letters seems to support a **rejection-replacement theology**. This is the belief that Paul repudiated his ancestral faith in favor of Christianity. Paul "rejected" the law and "replaced" it with the grace of Christ. I will discuss later whether this is an appropriate way to read Paul's letters in context, though, in some ways, it is a moot point. What we cannot debate is that Jewish communities have endured bigotry, terror, and violence for centuries because of the prevailing and popular ways Paul is interpreted. This is a sin and a shame.

Similarly, Paul is often depicted as a puritanical male chauvinist. His words reinforce gender hierarchies and sexual prohibitions. For example, Paul tells the church in Corinth that women should be silent in the churches (1 Cor. 14:34). The author of 1 Timothy, writing in Paul's name, declares that women should learn in silence and not be permitted to teach or have authority over men (1 Tim. 2:12). Many Catholic, Anglican, and Protestant leaders continue to appeal to these verses in order to prevent women from occupying positions of church leadership. Couple this with Paul's writings in Romans and Corinthians denouncing same-sex love, and it is clear why Paul's writings have become a scriptural resource of choice for those who denounce shifting views in our society about gender roles and sexuality. Christians who believe women should submit humbly to male authority and that same-sex desire is sinful find a theological ally in the apostle Paul. Over time he has become the premier authoritative voice supporting Christian, male, heterosexual supremacy. Paul, the unmarried frequent business traveler, somehow became the authority on appropriate domestic order.

Finally, there is the matter of slavery. Defenders of chattel slavery in the Americas appealed to the letters of Paul and to other letters that were commonly misattributed to him. In his letter to Philemon, Paul encourages kindness toward, but not the freedom of, Philemon's slave. In the voice of Paul, the writer of the Letter to Titus states, "Tell slaves to be submissive to their masters and to give satisfaction in every respect, never talk back, not to pilfer, but show complete and perfect fidelity" (Titus 2:9). And Ephesians 6:5 reads, "Slaves, obey your earthly masters with fear and trembling, in singleness of heart, as you obey Christ."

Renowned theologian Howard Thurman developed an oppositional relationship to Paul at an early age. In his autobiography, *With Head and Heart*, he tells of how it was his responsibility to read Scripture to his grandmother when he was a child. Whenever he would come to the letters of Paul, the formerly enslaved matriarch would ask him to skip over them. According to his grandmother, the minister approved by the plantation owner to preach each Sunday seemed to have only one text: "Slaves, obey your earthly masters." His grandmother vowed that if she could ever read Scripture on her own, she would ignore the writings of Paul. To Thurman's grandmother, like so many others, Paul signified enslavement and oppression rather than freedom and liberation.

Interpreted without its sociohistorical context, Paul's letters have bruised the humanity of countless Jews and Christians. People use his words to justify shunning women from church leadership, discriminating against people in same-sex relationships, and enslaving other human beings. This helps to explain why it is so important to engage Paul's epistles in context. As much as any other section of the Bible, Paul's letters have bruised the humanity of countless Jews and Christians. I would even argue that due to the genre of writing under consideration, the exegetical approach recommended in the second chapter is of even greater importance when considering the letters of Paul. Since we only have Paul's side of the conversations, we need to know something about the communities to which Paul was writing. Solid secondary sources can provide insight into the cultural setting, which, as we now know, helps to determine meaning. Hence, the sociohistorical approach enables us to better surmise Paul's purpose in writing, as well as what the communities may have received from his words.

## Reconsidering Paul

As a principal founder and organizer of Christian communities, Paul used letters to keep in touch with the people during his missionary journeys. These letters provide powerful insight into the growing strand of Judaism that came to be known as the Jesus movement in the latter half of the first century. Paul spent decades organizing churches along the strip of the Mediterranean that currently constitutes parts of southern Europe and western Asia. He wrote as a pastor to each congregation. Each letter is particular, written to a specific group and espousing his theology as relevant to a stated concern. No letter contains a broad exposition of his theology, although some letters are more comprehensive than others.

Because Paul's letters represent one side of a correspondence, we have to reconstruct carefully the context and cultural scripts that framed the apostle's responses. Anyone who has ever eavesdropped on one side of a conversation or intercepted an email reply without the original correspondence knows that partial details can create an incredible misunderstanding. Imagine catching a glimpse of a text message on your significant other's phone. I suspect you would be disturbed if you read, "I ❤ U! Can't wait to 👀 U!" This would surely lead to strong feelings of disappointment and betrayal. To discover that this message was sent by a parent or sibling, however, would alter the meaning and thus your interpretation. Without knowing the who, where, what, and why, we can string together random words and make them mean whatever we want. Context matters.

So is the case with Paul's letters. Understanding the context in which they were written will deter us from imposing whatever meaning we choose upon them, a flawed interpretive tactic known as eisegesis. Responsible exegesis, on the other hand, will provide us with more productive interpretations of Paul's aims. This is not to suggest that simply understanding Paul's letters in context will redeem Paul from all critiques. His writings are so covered by the blood of Christian triumphalism, sexism, and slavery that even the strongest "That's not what he meant" argument will not fully exonerate Paul of all charges against him. Good exegesis cannot undo nearly two millennia of harm. Our aim is not to "rescue" Paul from all criticism as much as it is to situate him within the appropriate social and historical context. By doing so, we might see how Paul exemplifies the same moral complexity and contradictions possessed by all pivotal characters throughout history.

The apostle Paul's dramatic conversion is among the more popular stories in the New Testament. The book of Acts introduces him as Saul, a zealous Jewish leader who was headed to the synagogues in Damascus to bring back Jews who were following the teachings of Jesus (9:1–2). On his way, he heard the voice of Jesus say, "Saul, Saul, why do you persecute me?" Immediately Saul went from being a persecutor to a promoter of Christ (9:3–9).

The powerful account of Paul's transformation has great significance in Christian communities. Paul appears to instantaneously convert from a bad man to a pious follower. This type of testimony is consistent with how many Christians, particularly evangelicals, think of conversion and salvation. A person once addicted to drugs and alcohol will often testify as to how "God removed the taste from my mouth" at the point of conversion. Others recall an immediate deliverance from negative behaviors in such a way that salvation is likened to a 180-degree turnaround. The account of Paul's conversion, then, provides many Christians with a vocabulary for salvation. Many feel like Paul at some point. The very moment that they were heading down a dangerous, crooked path to Damascus, Christ stepped in and directed them to "go to the street called Straight" (Acts 9:11).

Though this description of Paul's conversion makes sense in terms of his having a change of mind, there remains much confusion about what Paul was converting from. The conventional narrative is that Paul converted from Judaism to Christianity, from a life adhering to the law of Moses to salvation by way of the grace of Christ. Unfortunately, this view is as historically inaccurate as it is theologically insidious. It's historically inaccurate because it is based on an assumption that Judaism and Christianity were as distinguishable in the first century as they are today. In reality, the untethering of Christianity from Judaism was a protracted process. Theologians began to read the eventual split back into Paul's writings. This explains why such a Jewish to Christian conversion narrative is also theologically insidious. It makes false and insulting claims about Paul's relationship to his own tradition of Judaism. Anti-Semitism fermented and festered for hundreds of years. Tragically, these sorts of claims contributed to Adolf Hitler's genocidal "final solution" and still fuel white supremacy and anti-Semitism in the contemporary moment.

Evidently, we need another way to think about Paul. The best path forward is to attempt to reconstruct Paul's preconversion life. What can we decipher about Paul's upbringing? What can we know about Paul's religious background and training? What context shaped Paul's view of the world? Here we can proceed with our method of collecting clues from the materials that we have about Paul and his social world. These materials come from the book of Acts and his own letters.[1] For instance, we can conclude that Paul was most likely born around the same time as Jesus, right at the turn of the first century of the common era. The book of Acts tells us that Paul was from Tarsus, a cosmopolitan city in the northeast corner of the Mediterranean Basin, in modern-day Turkey. Tarsus was the capital of the province of Cilicia and a key site of culture and education in the Greco-Roman world.

Despite growing up in such a cosmopolitan, Hellenized culture, Paul was also very proud of his Jewish roots. In writing to the church in Philippi, he declared, "If anyone else has reason to be confident in the flesh, I have more: circumcised on the eighth day, a member of the people of Israel, of the tribe of Benjamin, a Hebrew born of Hebrews" (Phil. 3:4–5). Paul's references to circumcision, membership in the tribe of Benjamin, and being a "Hebrew born of Hebrews" underscore his Jewish bona fides. Yet like so many other Jews throughout the diaspora, Paul spoke the language of the Mediterranean region of the empire, Koine Greek. Paul's letters and writing style reveal that he was very familiar with the Greek translation of the Hebrew Bible known as the **Septuagint** (traditionally abbreviated LXX), from the Latin *septuaginta* ("seventy"). Its name derives from the tradition attributed to its origin. It is said that Egyptian ruler Ptolemy II sponsored the translation of the Hebrew Bible in the third century BCE and placed seventy Jewish scholars in individual rooms. Miraculously, all seventy produced identical wording of the Scripture. This is the translation to which Paul most commonly appeals.

These diverse dimensions of Paul's upbringing provide

---

1. There are many New Testament scholars, including my colleague Laura Nasrallah, who regard the Acts of the Apostles as an untrustworthy source for historical information regarding Paul. First, like the Pentateuch and Dynastic literature, Acts was written as sacred history and is full of grandiose embellishments. Second, Paul's own writings contradict some of the historical details recorded in Acts. Thus, it is better to rely on Paul's authenticated writings when attempting to reconstruct his life and times.

us with important insights about his early life. For one, they say something about the fluid cultures of the Greco-Roman Empire. There is little need to debate whether Paul was more informed by the Greek philosophical schools of the empire or by the moral and civic traditions of Judaism. This is a false debate. Jews living in cities like Tarsus were not wholly Hellenized, nor was Judea wholly Jewish. Both Jerusalem and the Jewish diaspora of Paul's day were more integrated than one might imagine. Hellenization began in Judea centuries earlier than Paul with the conquest of Alexander. Herod the Great's expansive building projects in the decades just preceding Jesus' birth were tributes to Rome. Judea had the empire's fingerprints all over it. During Jesus' life, it was possible to receive a Greek philosophical education in Jerusalem, and even Jewish elites in Jerusalem readily embraced the style and mannerisms of the Greco-Roman world.

Cultural influence was not a one-way street out of Rome. Jews also made a significant impact in large metropolitan cities of the empire. Jewish communities existed throughout the diaspora for hundreds of years prior to Paul. They established their own synagogues and held close to their traditions. In fact, it was common for non-Jews—referred to as "Gentiles" in the New Testament—to frequent synagogues. Many Gentiles respected the discipline and traditions of Jewish communities and sought to emulate Jewish observance, rituals, and practices. Jews referred to these Gentiles as "God-fearers." This includes other proselytes who converted to Judaism and embraced the Torah. Thus, when Paul began his ministry to the Gentiles, he did not need to search far for an audience. Many Gentiles were already gravitating toward the ethical teachings of the Torah.

This sort of cultural hybridity is an important point for us to remember as we consider the matter of Paul's so-called conversion. Throughout his life, Paul was a Jew involved in an internal religious debate with other Jews. There was no such thing as Christianity apart from Judaism in Paul's lifetime. In fact, Christianity and Judaism were difficult to distinguish in the

Mediterranean world as late as the fourth century. Christians observed the Sabbath on Saturday, and Easter and Passover coincided. Archaeological evidence also points to the common symbols used by Jews and Christians. Bread, wine, a cup, and fish symbols adorned the tombstones and houses of worship of both groups. It seems quite clear, then, that Judaism continued to serve as a meaningful and important spiritual tradition for many followers of Jesus for centuries following the apostle Paul's death.

## Reading with Someone Else's Eyes

Anyone who has ever been part of a community of faith knows how practices that might be accepted as normal among most people can ruffle the feathers of church leaders. Having clear control of the community is a way for church leaders to secure power. The same was true in the ancient world. As Christianity developed as a faith, the cultural synergy between Christianity and Judaism frustrated the efforts of Christian leaders to claim independent, authoritative voices within their communities— the sort of authority that could yield both cultural and economic capital for religious leaders. Unfortunately, attempts to untether Christianity from its parent faith were often expressed with virulent, anti-Jewish sentiment that has continued to the present moment.

Among the earliest Christian leaders who sought to facilitate the split was theologian Marcion of Sinope (85–160 CE) in the mid-second century. Marcion believed that Christianity was incompatible with Judaism, and thus he opposed the writings of the Hebrew Bible. He was among the earliest to introduce a Christian canon, which included the Gospel of Luke and the Letters of Paul. Consistent with his theological views, he removed all passages from Luke and the Epistles that appeared to show any continuity between Judaism and Christianity. Marcion lost this battle among other early Christian groups. Few were comfortable denying the impact of the

Hebrew Bible on the Christian faith. Still, Marcion may have won the ultimate war. His canon helped shape what church leaders distinguished as the New Testament, which subordinated the writings of the Hebrew Bible to the Old Testament. Christianity became a "new" Israel that superseded the "old."

In the late fourth century, Archbishop John Chrysostom preached and wrote against Christians who continued to adopt Jewish observances and traditions. Chrysostom was born in Antioch, the cradle of early Christianity. According to the book of Acts, this is the city where members of the Jesus movement were first called Christians. Chrysostom was known for his eloquent preaching, ascetic lifestyle, and commitment to the poor; the name Chrysostom is actually an epithet meaning "golden mouthed." Yet he was also known for his invectives against Christians who celebrated traditional Jewish festivals and worshiped alongside Jews in Antioch. Chrysostom's violent and vicious "Homilies against the Jews" described Jewish synagogues as brothels and its members as drunkards and gluttons. Writing in opposition to Christians who sought medical treatments within synagogues, Chrysostom employed the slur "Christ killers" and spoke of his own desire to take up arms against the Jews in Antioch.

This unfortunate and tragic tradition of anti-Semitism within Christian theology flourished over the next thousand years. Protestant Reformers such as Martin Luther picked it up with reckless enthusiasm. Luther's 1543 treatise "On the Jews and Their Lies" describes Jews with violent, gendered language. Terms like "whoring" and "slut" are common, and he likens Jewish confidence in the law to a "beautiful woman without discretion," citing Proverbs 11:22. He goes on to add, "Therefore, this boast about the external laws of Moses, apart from obedience to the Ten Commandments, should be silenced; indeed, this boast makes the Jews seven times more unworthy to be God's people than the Gentiles are. For the external laws were not given to make a nation the people of God, but to adorn and enhance God's people externally." Among the many stories of Christianity, one does predominate: from early church fathers such as Marcion to the Protestant Reformers in the sixteenth century, to embrace Christianity is to reject (violently) Judaism.

This tradition of anti-Semitism creates a problem for how we read the letters of Paul in context. We interpret Paul's letters with the cultural CliffsNotes of these later Christian theologians. Whether we realize it or not, we see the scribbled notes of John Chrysostom, Martin Luther, and so many others in the margins of Paul's letters. This informs how we read Paul. The concerns, biases, and bigotries of later Christians get mapped back on to the apostle. Then we read Paul's challenges to his critics and defenses of his own theological position as something quite different from what the apostle may have intended. It is easy for the casual reader to believe that Paul was a convert from Judaism to Christianity and that he rejected the law of Moses and other Jewish customs such as circumcision outright. If for almost two thousand years most Christian theologians have framed Christianity in opposition to or a "fulfillment" of Judaism, then clearly Paul did too, right? Wrong. This is what I am afraid happens when we read someone else's mail with the wrong eyes and flawed assumptions.

### One in Christ

Beyond setting Paul within his historical context, it will prove helpful for us to identify some major themes in the apostle's letters. Traditionally there are thirteen letters assumed to belong to Paul: 1 and 2 Thessalonians, Galatians, 1 and 2 Corinthians, Philemon, Philippians, Romans, Colossians, Ephesians, 1 and 2 Timothy, and Titus. That seven of these belong to Paul is indisputable: 1 Thessalonians, Galatians, 1 and 2 Corinthians, Philemon, Philippians, and Romans. Each was written during the sixth decade of the first century, at least a decade before the earliest known Gospel (Mark). We suspect that the other letters were written pseudonymously under Paul's name. The distinction is a matter of consistency. Scholars well-versed in Koine Greek look for certain patterns in rhetorical style, vocabulary, and themes. Paul, for instance, often refers to the "the heavens" in his letters. The Letter to the Ephesians speaks of "heavenly places." This is why some dispute whether Paul is the author. The same can be said of Paul's consistent use of the noun *kyrios* ("lord") to describe those who own slaves. Yet in 1 Timothy and Titus, the author uses the noun *despotes* ("master"). This sort of deviation in language leads scholars to believe that the latter two epistles are not Paul's.

Second, alongside language, there are a few consistent themes in Paul's epistles. Consider Paul's notion of the "oneness" of the body of Christ. In several instances, Paul claims that Christ unites believers who live according to the spirit and reject the flesh. The spirit, for Paul, represents an ideal essence for those who have been reborn in Christ. Life in the spirit leads to unity and oneness in the body of Christ. This is the model of community that Paul promotes with passion and vigor throughout the epistles.

Historian Daniel Boyarin argues powerfully that Paul's understanding of oneness was actually derived from an influential Greek philosophical concept of the day. According to this school of thought, cultural difference worked against the highest ideals of the moral life. Elevation of the moral mind means transcending the body. In applying this concept to life in Christ, Paul came to believe that any cultural distinction that might frustrate the full inclusion of anyone into the household of God ought to be rejected. Believers in Christ became one in the spirit of Christ, but cultural signs of difference represented "the flesh." Any social marker, including those that created hierarchies of privilege, worked against Paul's community-building efforts.

This spiritual vision had social and political impact. Appeals to oneness in the spirit allowed Paul's hearers to reimagine social hierarchy. Any physical and social markers of difference that might privilege some while excluding others ran counter to life in Christ. Let's look at the Letter to the Galatians. Here Paul is upset that some other apostles within the Jesus movement have convinced members of the congregation to accept circumcision and other aspects of the Mosaic law. An irate Paul writes, "You foolish Galatians! Who has bewitched you?" (3:1) This is clearly a rhetorical question, since Paul has already identified three of his opponents by name: James, Peter, and John, leaders of the Jesus movement in Jerusalem (Gal. 2:12).

Obviously, the original disciples of Jesus did not agree with Paul. They believed that Gentiles within the Jesus movement should observe certain practices to which Jesus adhered. Since Paul's opponents in Galatia were teaching under the authority of James, Jesus' brother, Paul found himself on the defensive. This may explain why Paul spends so much time defending his own authority in the first two chapters of the Letter to the Galatians. The apostle notes how he received the full approval of James and others, but these men were now going back on their promise. The problem, Paul asserts, is not with his own teachings but with any apostles who view themselves as distinct from the Gentiles due to their observance of the law.

What we have, then, is a conflict between Paul and other apostles of the Jesus movement. Paul is not denouncing the faith of the Jewish apostles. If we follow the book of Acts, he is simply trying to get them to adhere to a previous agreement settled at the Council of Jerusalem. As this agreement is written in Acts 15:19–20, "We should not trouble those Gentiles who are turning to God, but we should write to them to abstain only from things polluted by idols and from fornication and from whatever has been strangled and from blood."

This type of reading of Galatians is different from more traditional and anti-Semitic rejection-replacement interpretations. Paul is not rejecting the law for Jews. Nor is he suggesting that their religious tradition ought to be supplanted. Paul's concern is ensuring Gentile inclusion in God's promises to Israel. Paul's concept of oneness in Galatians, then, explains how Paul attempts to lift any barrier that could exclude Gentiles from the faith of Abraham. Paul's discontent was not with Judaism but with the strategies of his apostolic colleagues for how Gentiles ought to be included. He felt that requiring Jewish rituals such as circumcision for membership in the Jesus movement was too high and would possibly create internal hierarchies within the movement. As he famously wrote to the Galatians, "There is no longer Jew or Greek, there is no longer slave or free, there is no longer male and female; for all of you are one in Christ Jesus. And if you belong to Christ, then you are Abraham's offspring, heirs according to the promise" (3:28–29). One can imagine how those in the churches who experienced relative levels of social exclusion based on gender, ability, poverty, or ethnicity might find Paul's emphasis on unity attractive.

Alongside Paul's emphasis on oneness in Galatians is another noteworthy feature of Paul's thinking. Paul's letters are replete with bondage and liberation metaphors and analogies. In Romans, Paul says that he is "of the flesh, sold into slavery under sin" (7:14). Paul seemed to believe that all of humanity was enslaved to sin (6:6). Elsewhere Paul contends that Christ, who was equal to God, emptied himself by "taking the form of a slave, being born in human likeness" (Phil. 2:7) And when providing instruction regarding what members of the Corinthian church can and cannot do with their bodies, Paul writes, "Do you not know that your body is a temple of the Holy Spirit within you, which you have from God, and that you are not your own? For you were bought with a price; therefore glorify God in your body" (1 Cor. 6:19–20).

It should not surprise us that Paul relies so heavily on the imagery of slavery. Slavery was such a staple of Roman imperial life that the image of freedom from bondage would certainly resonate with a cross section of society. Of the sixty million people who constituted the Roman Empire, historians estimate that about twelve million, or up to 20 percent, were enslaved. Some have even argued that Paul was either enslaved or a direct descendant of the enslaved himself. There is a long tradition going back to Jerome in the fourth century that maintains this position. Features of Paul's upbringing such as his having received a philosophical education and the skill of leather working would have meant that Paul had a patron to subsidize the cost of education and professional training, a patron such as a slaveholder. Whatever the case may be, it is hard to ignore that slavery and freedom provided a framework for Paul to think about how society is structured. Conversely, it provided the framework to think about how society could be restructured for those who desired to be set free by embracing a "life in Christ," namely, those living on the underside of social inequality.

## A Politics of Difference

Paul's image of oneness in Christ and allusions to liberation from bondage paint a beautiful picture of radical equality. His spiritual visions had concrete social implications for the most vulnerable. It seems safe to conclude that this was not Paul's purpose, however. Nowhere in the apostle's writings does he come off as willing to embrace the political consequences of his otherworldly rhetoric. If Paul is encouraging members of the Jesus movement to ignore the pains, problems, and perplexities of this world in hope of a better world to come, he may be asking believers to acquiesce to injustice and capitulate to oppression.

Consider these examples. We noted above that Paul argues in his letter to the Galatians that in Christ the socially constructed categories of male and female are erased. Yet in 1 Corinthians, Paul contends that women should cease speaking out and asking questions in church and instead receive instruction from their husbands at home (14:34–35). Paul argues in Romans 6 that in Christ we are all set free from the bondage of sin and should become only slaves of God. When it came to the actual system of slavery in the ancient world, however, Paul's letter to Philemon reveals that he was not willing to defy the culture of slavery in order to assist the enslaved Onesimus in gaining his physical freedom. Paul's characterizations of life in the spirit did not translate to life in the actual real world.

There are two ways to read Paul in this regard. On the one hand, we can view him as a tactical church builder, one who became, in his words, "all things to all people, that I might by all means save some" (1 Cor. 9:22). Paul conceded to Realpolitik where it would help his mission efforts. Maybe Paul would have preferred for all cultural distinctions, including hierarchies of male/female and free/slave, to be erased. But he was aware of the cultural and political pressures that these vulnerable communities of faith faced. Christian communities in cities such as Corinth were increasingly viewed with suspicion and derision by their pagan neighbors. Paul's teachings on radical equality would have certainly garnered unwanted attention from the movement's opponents. Maybe gender equality and slavery's abolition were battles that Paul was not willing to fight. Maybe proposing a model of benevolent domination for marriage and servitude for the Christians in cities such as Corinth were Paul's compromises. He would teach this otherworldly vision of God's kingdom while having members of the Jesus movement blend into the structures of society.

On the other hand, maybe Paul was so convinced that the end time was near that short-term concessions were not necessary. He may have believed that social arrangements and human relations were passing away (1 Cor. 7:31). Thus, he may have felt it was best for members of the Jesus movement to prepare to witness Christ's return. Differences will not matter when believers stand before God. Nor will social status be of importance to those expecting the apocalypse. This is why the social and political implications of Paul's teachings did not seem to matter to the apostle. Paul was concerned with another kingdom, not this one.

Paul's intentions, however, only tell part of the story. Recall our discussion in the first chapter about the interpretive process. People hear messages differently based on their context. One's location in the social order surely informed how figuratively or literally one received Paul's message. Paul might have intended for listeners to receive a uniform message about life in the spirit in preparation for Christ's return. This would not stop people from applying his teachings on equality before God to their personal lives. Imagine yourself a widow bound by the cultural conventions of patriarchy and limited social mobility. Conceive of yourself as enslaved and wholly dependent on an owner. To hear Paul say, "There is no longer Jew or Greek, there is no longer slave or free, there is no longer male and female," is certainly a message you would welcome.

Several women in the early Jesus movement did take Paul's eradication of male gender hierarchy literally. In Romans, we are introduced to several of Paul's ministry partners, such as Phoebe, a deacon of the church at Cenchreae (Rom. 16:1). There are Priscilla and Aquila, a married couple who traveled alongside the apostle. Priscilla's name is often mentioned first, which bucks the conventional writing formula and speaks to Priscilla's status (16:3). There is reason to believe that Priscilla was considered the more capable teacher and preacher of the gospel. There is also Junia, who was imprisoned with Paul. He describes her as "prominent among the apostles" (16:7). And the book of Acts introduces Lydia of Thyatira, who sold purple linen, a color reserved for the wealthy (Acts 16:14). We know that she supported Paul and Timothy, even hosting them in her home. There is never a mention of a man in relation to Lydia, which gives us reason to believe that she controlled her own business and household and, hence, supported Paul with her own resources.

These examples provide grounds to reject the most common interpretation of 1 Corinthians 14:34–35, the two verses that have been used to sanction the silencing and subjugation of women in our churches. Here the apostle writes, "Women should be silent in the churches. For they are not permitted to speak, but should be subordinate, as the law also says. If there is anything they desire to know, let them ask their husbands at

home." Rather than conceding that, as in all of his other epistles, Paul was providing instructions on how to deal with particular women within the Corinthian congregation, advocates
of male supremacy universalize Paul's words. They expand his
contextually located prohibition against certain women and
apply it to all women. Such perverse interpretations ignore
Paul's actual ministry practices that depended on the leadership of women. The Bible, then, becomes more like a butcher's
knife that hacks off the importance of women in the establishment and growth of the Jesus movement.

Women such as Lydia and Phoebe were not the only ones
who heard a message of liberation and social opportunity in
Paul's teaching. There was Onesimus. We learn about him in
Paul's letter to Philemon. Like all of Paul's letters, Philemon
should be read in its entirety. From this letter, we can gather
that Onesimus was enslaved in Philemon's household and had
come to know Paul during the apostle's time in their city. Quite
possibly both Philemon and Onesimus became members of
the Jesus movement under Paul's influence. The letter reveals
that Onesimus has fled Philemon's household and sought out
Paul to help the apostle expand the ministry. Some scholars
have likened Onesimus to a "runaway slave."

We do not know why Onesimus fled. Historians tell us that it
was common for the enslaved in Greco-Roman society to flee
in order to look for a new patron. In contrast to the enslaved
in the Americas many centuries later, the enslaved in Greco-
Roman society were often highly educated and skilled in professions. Slaves worked as business managers, accountants, and
even physicians for wealthy patrons. Moreover, since slavery
was not race-based, slaves could move freely through society.
Many would take advantage of their skills to identify another
patron if irreconcilable differences ever arose between slave
and slaveholder. This appears to be Onesimus's aim in the letter. Whether he made a financial mistake within Philemon's
household that would warrant severe punishment or he just
woke up one day and decided that he wanted his freedom, we

do not know. What we do know is that Paul writes a letter to Philemon requesting that he take Onesimus back.

If we read this letter from Paul's perspective, it may appear that the apostle is doing a noble deed on multiple fronts. For instance, Paul encourages Philemon to take Onesimus back and hit the reset button on the relationship. He hopes Philemon might forgive Onesimus of any past infractions, including possible financial malfeasance. This is why Paul tells Philemon to "charge that to my account" if Onesimus owes him anything (v. 18). Paul even goes a step further and reaffirms his teachings concerning the eradication of difference. He asks Philemon to be gentle with Onesimus and to treat him like a brother instead of a slave (v. 16). By sending Onesimus back to Philemon, Paul was honoring Roman policy. Since it was difficult to tell who was free or enslaved, fugitive slave laws could be severe for those harboring runaways. The system of patron exchange and financial compensation depended on the wealthy honoring this code of conduct. By sending Onesimus back with this letter, Paul both reaffirms his teachings on freedom in Christ and upholds Roman law.

But what happens when we put on our lenses of love? That the enslaved Onesimus is the most vulnerable person in the text is pretty evident. Nor do I suspect that Onesimus regards Paul's decision to send him back to his master as an honorable act. Let's imagine the combination of courage, desperation, and hope that it probably took Onesimus to confront Paul with his request. I can envision Onesimus reciting back to Paul some of the apostle's own teachings.

Maybe Onesimus said, "I heard your sermon where you said that Adam was the first man who inaugurated sin in the world. This is why we are all trapped in bondage to sin. But Christ is the second Adam who breaks the chains of sin" (Rom. 5:12–18). Maybe Onesimus recalled the sermon where Paul declared that to live in Christ is to be a new creature no longer marked Jew or Gentile, slave or free, but liberated by the power of Jesus' resurrection (Gal. 3:28; 2 Cor. 5:17). And maybe Onesimus complained to Paul: "I received your gospel of Christ, and Philemon says that he received it. He leads the church in his home every week and talks about Christ setting us all free. Yet he still whips me harshly and threatens to kill me if I do not obey his commands."

What is clear is that Onesimus wanted to be treated as a brother in Christ, not a slave in bondage. This is why it is hard for me to imagine anything other than Onesimus walking away defeated and dejected. He came to Paul looking for freedom. He came seeking to live out the liberation that Paul taught him can be found in Christ. He received a letter to his master that essentially said, "Play nice."

Though Paul taught about freedom, his moral imagination would not allow him to conceive of a world that was truly free of the master-slave system. Paul preached about eradicating social distinctions. He painted theological visions of Christ embracing bondage to sin in order to deliver us. Yet when given the chance, Paul conceded to convention. When given the opportunity to help just one enslaved man, Onesimus, it appears that the enormity of the injustice of slavery overwhelmed Paul. In more ways than one, then, Paul's letters teach us important though contrasting lessons about spiritual life and ethical living. On the one hand, they teach us the importance of envisioning a new social order where we affirm the humanity and equality of all of God's children. On the other hand, they show us the importance of seeking to live out and enact the social worlds we envision. It is not enough to preach and pray. We must also work to protect the vulnerable and protest injustice. In my view, this is what it means to be "in Christ."

**For Further Reading**

Boyarin, Daniel. *A Radical Jew: Paul and the Politics of Identity.* Berkeley: University of California Press, 1994.

Gager, John G. *Reinventing Paul.* New York: Oxford University Press, 2002.

Gager, John G. *The Origins of Anti-Semitism: Attitudes toward Judaism in Pagan and Christian Antiquity.* New York: Oxford University Press, 1985.

Glancy, Jennifer A. *Slavery in Early Christianity.* Minneapolis: Fortress Press, 2006.

Glancy, Jennifer A. *Slavery as a Moral Problem in the Early Church and Today.* Minneapolis: Fortress Press, 2011.

Johnson, Matthew V., James A. Noel, and Demetrius K. Williams, eds. *Onesimus Our Brother: Reading Religion, Race, and Culture in Philemon.* Minneapolis: Fortress Press, 2012.

Nasrallah, Laura. *Archaeology and the Letters of Paul.* New York: Oxford University Press, forthcoming.

Neyrey, Jerome H. *Paul, in Other Words: A Cultural Reading of His Letters.* Louisville, KY: Westminster/John Knox Press, 1990.

Osiek, Carolyn, Margaret Y. MacDonald, and Janet H. Tulloch. *A Woman's Place: House Churches in Early Christianity.* Minneapolis: Fortress Press, 2006.

Stendahl, Krister. *Paul among Jews and Gentiles*, and Other Essays. Philadelphia: Fortress Press, 1976.

# 9

## Faith over Fear

## A New Testament Ethic of Resistance

> There is no fear in love, but perfect love casts out fear.
> —1 John 4:18

> Fear is the path to the dark side. Fear leads to anger.
> Anger leads to hate. Hate leads to suffering.
> —Yoda the Jedi master

In chapter 7 we saw that the Gospels subvert conventional power and traditional wisdom. Jesus' parables invite readers into a mystical world wherein society's so-called winners and losers are inverted. And miracle accounts challenge prevailing purity politics of the day, common understandings of behaviors society considered holy or defiled. Miracles encourage followers to see themselves as God views them, as healthy and whole. Similarly, in chapter 8 we saw that Paul's emphasis on oneness in the body of Christ in his letter to the Galatians disrupted cultural borders and social boundaries. Even if Paul had only the end time in mind, hearers such as the enslaved Onesimus quite possibly heard a cultural challenge and critique. Heavenly visions of a world without class hierarchy and slavery had this-worldly implications for those who sought freedom from oppression.

Social divisions that existed in the ancient world such as between Jews and Samaritans, rich and poor, and pure and impure are much like many boundaries that exist between groups in our society. Interrelated factors such as religion, race, ethnicity, sexuality, and socioeconomic status create our own forms of purity politics that rival those of the ancient world. These social boundaries become ways for those in power groups to marginalize, ostracize, villainize, and criminalize others based on little more than physical markers.

In the United States, Muslims are bearing the weight of our ignorance and fear. A young Muslim boy was accused of bringing a bomb to school when he had just built a clock for science class. A college student was removed from a flight for speaking Arabic on a telephone call with his uncle. Three Muslim students at the University of North Carolina at Chapel Hill were murdered by a crazed gunman who felt "threatened." In 2017, U.S. president Donald J. Trump signed an executive order that placed a travel ban on all seeking to enter the country from seven majority Muslim countries. Federal agents have interrogated and detained numerous travelers, students, and dual citizens at airports in recent months. As I write, the travel ban continues to make its way through the courts to assess its constitutionality. However, it is clear that this executive order has widespread support from the American public.

Some cite terrorist attacks carried out in the name of Allah in order to justify racial profiling and other discriminatory acts toward those of Arab descent. This is a specious argument, since 64 percent of mass shootings in the United States since 1982 have been carried out by white males. Yet few refer to Dylann Roof, the white, Confederate-flag-donning young man who murdered nine African American worshipers inside Emmanuel African Methodist Episcopal Church in Charleston, South Carolina, as a "radical American terrorist." When violence is at the hands of white men, they are often described as people with problems. When members of minoritized communities inflict violence, they represent a problem people. The former are framed as unique, a violent anomaly to the norm. The latter are framed as representative of the whole.

Throughout this book, I have sought to demonstrate that the social problems and ethical dilemmas we face in our world today are not very different in scale from those that faced biblical writers. Injustice can feel so enormous and overwhelming that we do not know where to begin. Moral truths get buried under the deceptions of our daily practices. As Paul was unable to challenge the system of slavery in his letter to Philemon, we find it easy to become blinded by the way things are. Our moral vision is lost. Our moral imaginations are short-circuited. Rather than striving to realize God's will of peace and justice "on earth as it is in heaven," we resign ourselves to prevailing forces. Whenever injustice comes across as inevitable and intractable, even the most committed can lose faith.

We have employed the sociohistorical approach to interpret the Bible. By examining the social and historical context of the world in which the Bible was produced, we are better able to consider how the ancients imagined and interpreted writings about God. Understanding the appropriate cultural cues that shaped meaning helps us to read the Bible in its world so that we might responsibly appropriate visions of love and justice in our world. There are many biblical accounts in which God privileges those whom society otherwise ignores. The method of interpretation we have employed throughout this book—putting on the lenses of love—searches for the people and perspectives that social custom, cultural power, and theological convention have silenced. We want to see the ones God sees—the least, the left out, and the left behind.

I want to extend that method in this final chapter. First, I want us to consider how social divisions and hierarchies were maintained in Jesus' world so that we might identify particular ways in which we maintain injustice in our world. One way that I wish to note is the explosion of the prison industrial complex in the United States. Jesus brought a message of peace and justice to a world marked by institutional violence and structural inequality. What might his message say to us? Far from Jesus' politics of compassion, over the past fifty years, the United States has turned to a program of mass imprisonment in order to contain populations that this nation would rather keep out of sight and mind. Prisons have become a way to ostracize and contain the social lepers and Samaritans among us.

Second, I want to imagine how we as people of faith might deploy our moral imagination to address another ethical dilemma confronting church and society in the United States: the gun culture. America's fascination with guns is neither normal nor natural. The epidemic of gun violence renders us an outlier in the developed world. What is more, despite popular narratives that correlate guns and freedom with the founding fathers of this nation, gun culture is a more recent development that began in the twentieth century with a comprehensive marketing campaign by the gun industry. This may be why so many people believe that any sort of gun regulation is an anathema to American identity. Like slavery in Paul's day, guns are just part of the social fabric that too many of us take for granted. Yet is there a word from the Lord to help us speak up and speak out against this particular form of idolatry?

### From Peasant to Bandit

Jesus was born into a world marked by violence and political oppression. This was a result of the series of empires that ruled the region. Galilee and Judea experienced colonial rule by the Assyrians, Babylonians, Persians, Greeks, and Romans. At the time of Jesus' birth, Jews in Palestine lived under a client state system; their local leaders were politically and economically subservient to Roman officials. Priests headquartered in the temple in Jerusalem reported to an appointed client king who enforced the will of the empire. The most infamous client king of the era was Herod the Great, who appears in the Gospels.

Historians disagree on how to view the effects of this political system controlled by local puppet leaders. In his classic *The Historical Figure of Jesus*, E. P. Sanders describes this period of foreign rule in Palestine as relatively peaceful, although peace in relation to empire is always little more than a euphemism for stability enforced by violence. In his book *Jesus and the Politics of Roman Palestine*, historian Richard Horsley compares the imperial powers of ancient Rome to the brutality of European colonial movements of the nineteenth and twentieth centuries. He argues convincingly that empires always fear that subjugated peoples will one day revolt. Hence, peace, even from the perspective of those in power, is insecure at best.

Historical evidence verifies the Roman Empire's use of the specter of military violence as a form of terror and social control. Large-scale military parades served as imperial public theater. The intent was both to celebrate and to intimidate. The emperor and high-ranking officials would declare the *euangelion* (Greek for "gospel" or "good news") throughout the provinces. Thus, the successful conquest of new lands or squelching of resistance within a territory was announced as the *euangelion* of the emperor. The *euangelion* of Caesar Augustus instilled fear in some and devotion in others.

Inscriptions found on coins also capture how the peace of the empire was maintained with violence. The name of the Roman goddess of peace, Pax, was engraved on one side, with an image of the emperor holding a spear on the other. Peace and military might were literally two sides of the same coin. The sword maintained *Pax Romana*—the peace of Rome. Hence, Roman officials referred to Caesar Augustus as *soter*, Greek for "savior." For the Mediterranean masses, Augustus's sword was sharp and swift. He could trample trouble beneath his imperial feet. For some, he rescued them and brought them a new way. In the minds of many, Caesar Augustus was the savior of the world.

Augustus and his officials used crucifixion as an act and symbol to stamp out trouble. Anyone viewed as an insurrectionist was nailed to a cross and endured a slow and painful death. Crucifixion had two purposes: to punish political dissidents and to send a warning to all who might consider rebellion. Theologian James Cone likens crucifixion to the act of lynching in the American South. In *The Cross and the Lynching Tree*, Cone argues that beyond being a tool to foster fear among the oppressed, crucifixions, like lynching, were often accompanied by beatings, body dismemberment, and prolonged suffocation. Jews were nailed to crosses and their bodies publicly displayed to terrify anyone with the slightest thought of rebellion or dissent. In his first-century work *The War of the Jews*, historian Josephus describes Rome's response to uprisings that precipitated the Jewish war in Jerusalem around 66 CE. It was Rome's hope that "the sight of it [mass crucifixion] would perhaps induce the Jews to surrender in order to avoid the same fate. The soldiers themselves through rage and bitterness nailed up their victims in various attitudes as a grim joke until, owing to the vast numbers there was no room for crosses, and no crosses for the bodies." In short, to paraphrase Billie Holliday's sorrowful song about lynchings in the American South, Roman trees bore strange fruit.

Invariably, a climate of abuse and persecution from above cultivated increased resistance from below. Jesus' home region of Galilee was known as a hotbed of resistance. Roman officials labeled peasant dissidents from Galilee as "bandits," political and religious subversives who threatened the *Pax Romana*. (According to the Gospels, Jesus was crucified alongside two bandits.) Unfortunately, this label of political resistance has been lost over time, and now *bandit* is indistinguishable from *thief*. Yet banditry was far from petty criminality. Bandits were self-professed freedom fighters who were thorns in the side of the Judean religious elite, and they were forced to endure the constant surveillance of imperial officials. The fact that Jesus suffered this torturous death, then, says something about the company he kept. It also says something about how the empire sought to control and contain those considered a threat to the social order.

## Politics of Mass Imprisonment

The purity politics of ancient Palestine reveals much about who and what that society viewed as clean or dirty. This purity politics categorized people, established social boundaries, and created privilege. Unfortunately, more often than not, the poor and disaffected were the ones deemed unclean and impure. Those like Jesus who did not embrace the mores of the empire were most likely to be deemed bandits. In the context of empire, poverty and political resistance proved a sure path to imprisonment.

Unfortunately, it is not hard to identify similar systems of structural violence in our world today. Think about how the United States has elected to deal with the "unclean" among us. Economic policies that place corporate profits over people have invariably created surplus populations of the socially disaffected in the United States. Economists often refer to this group of people as "discouraged workers," those who experience unemployment for a long period or who opt for nontraditional and even underground forms of employment. They are not even counted in labor statistics that report unemployment rates. Some have failed to earn a high school degree and can find little opportunity in America's postindustrial economy. Chronic illness; disability; divorce; racial, religious, or gender discrimination; diminished wages; and escalating housing and childcare costs push people into the pool of the socially disaffected.

In a development over the past fifty years that is far from Jesus' politics of compassion, the United States has turned to a program of mass imprisonment in order to contain these populations. In his book *Lockdown America*, Christian Parenti notes that the prison industrial complex has become this nation's preferred way of dealing with those our society has deemed "social junk." Prisons reaffirm the class, racial, and gender hierarchies that help maintain pristine, privatized spaces of exclusion. In the final three decades of the twentieth century, the prison population in the United States expanded from around three hundred thousand to over two million. Hardly a result of increased crime, the increase was a consequence of tactical decisions and carefully constructed laws. Crime rates in the United States have remained virtually identical to those in Finland and Germany since 1970, but the rates of incarceration in those countries have either dropped or remained consistent. Instead, the United States has an incarceration rate that is anywhere from six to ten times greater than any other industrialized nation, to the point that it imprisons a half million more people than China despite having an overall population five times less. Mass imprisonment has become this nation's most efficient tool to enforce an unjust politics of purity.

Dangerously efficient and unjustly effective methods of mass imprisonment are a lucrative enterprise. Local municipalities and law enforcement officials receive great financial benefit. The privatized prison industrial complex is a multibillion-dollar industry. Corrections Corporation of America and the Geo Group, the two largest private (though publicly traded) detention companies, each records over a billion dollars of revenue annually. This sort of cash flow can have an inordinate influence on federal and state governments to incentivize policies that ensure private prison facilities remain occupied. Incarceration rates increased exponentially when the criminal justice system began to respond to low-threat drug possession, public-order offenses, and even nonpayment of associated court fees with jail time. In addition, working class, disproportionately black and brown neighborhoods were targeted with policing tactics such as "stop and frisk" in order to arrest young people on drug offenses—though I am confident drug arrests would be much higher if police practiced stop and frisk on any elite university campus in this nation. The tail of untoward intentions and unjust profits are wagging the dog of criminal justice in this nation. The prison industry has perverted the business of incarceration into a sick and twisted "field of dreams" for its beneficiaries. If they build the jails, "law and order" governments will help keep them full.

As destructive and unjust as the United States' preoccupation with prisons has been over the past fifty years, the blueprint as a way to handle America's "undesirables"—especially African Americans—was created much earlier. Following the Civil War, southern states began to use systems of crime and punishment to reinstitute the racial caste system that slavery enforced. A provision built into the Thirteenth Amendment outlaws slavery, "except as a punishment for crime." Immediately southern states started instituting "Black Codes" that outlawed petty offenses such as vagrancy, loitering, drunkenness, and simply being in the wrong place after dark. Alongside laws that restricted African American mobility, mass imprisonment became another way to mark unwanted bodies. But when the civil rights movement helped to outlaw segregation as a means of ostracizing those society considered dirty and defiled by virtue of their skin, the prison system stepped in to take up the slack. After the civil rights movement, the prison industrial complex instituted a different type of social hierarchy informed by race, which Michelle Alexander describes in her aptly titled book, *The New Jim Crow*.

It is beyond time for our country, and our churches, to seek a more just and merciful way to address a hurting humanity. The profit-driven criminal justice industry is unsustainable, untenable, and, most of all, unfit for a so-called healthy democracy. If we believe that we need more jails to keep us safe from one another, then we are already locked up. If we need more prisons to maintain peace, than we have predicated our peace upon tyranny and terrorizing the most vulnerable among us. And most importantly, this culture of mass imprisonment and order established by a police state has transformed the role of

police officers from protecting and serving citizens into crimi-
nalizing and containing those considered impure.

As an African American man, this outrages me. As a father
of two African American boys, this scares me. And as someone who knows what it is like to experience police officers who
know how to protect and serve, as well as those who view me
with fear and disdain, the politics driving a culture of mass
imprisonment saddens me.

Two contrasting stories make my point. I now live on a
campus where as a tenured professor and head of Harvard
University's Memorial Church, I know what it feels like to
be protected and served by the police. My daughter looks up
to Officer Thomas Howie and playfully tells her friends that
he is her "personal security team." Along with Officer Josiah
Christian and other members of the Harvard University Police
Department, I can always count on them to check on the house
when I travel, respond with poise and grace in the rare case
that there is a problem at my home or church, and greet me
each Monday morning with a hug, a smile, and a joke about my
beloved Atlanta Falcons.

Yet I know the other, more dangerous, side. A few years ago,
I served as a groomsman in a wedding in Little Rock, Arkansas.
Several alums of Morehouse and Spelman Colleges, two prominent historically black colleges in Atlanta, flew in from across
the country to celebrate with our classmates. About ten of us
were leaving our hotel parking lot to caravan to the rehearsal
dinner when two of the cars accidentally collided. We got out
of our cars and called the police in order to get a police report
for the drivers' insurance companies. A few minutes later a
couple of police cars pulled up, and the officers jumped out
with guns drawn. They yelled for us to get our hands on the
roof of the cars. These officers were not responding to our call,
but rather to the call of a hotel guest who reported a "gang
fight" in the parking lot.

It is important to note that there were several physicians
in the group. A few of us, including myself, were enrolled in

doctoral programs at the time, and there was a Wall Street executive and a school principal in our party. Nobody was drunk, there were no sagging pants, and there was no loud music coming from the cars. I say this solely to deflect the often asinine retort that if kids of color would simply pull up their pants and speak with respect to authority, they would not have problems with the police. But it was not a matter of personal appearance, education, or pedigree. The politics of respectability, meaning our ability to conform to the style of dress and behavior that the dominant society deems as appropriate, did not protect us. Having seen a group of ten African American men in the parking lot of a luxury hotel (without a visible "team bus" transporting us), someone decided that our bodies were occupying a space that defied the optical politics of who belonged where. And in the mind of the person who made that call and to the police officers who showed up on the scene, we were already criminals—mere thugs who could have lost our lives with one wrong move.

Such contrasting personal interactions with police officers should lead me neither to defend nor to demonize all officers. In fact, they strengthen my resolve to call out this dangerous trajectory that is endangering and dehumanizing every one of us. We cannot have "officers of the peace" clad in military fatigues armed with assault rifles as appears to be increasingly the case in America's cities. This is nothing more than a particular form of purity politics run amok. We can do better. The Gospels demand that we do better.

## Politics of Mass Murder

In December 2015, a married couple of Pakistani descent walked into a Christmas party at the San Bernardino County (Calif.) Department of Public Health. They were each armed with several semiautomatic weapons and handheld bombs. Within minutes, fourteen people were dead and twenty-two injured. According to a report compiled by the *PBS NewsHour* and based on the website Mass Shooting Tracker, this was one of 372 mass shootings that took place in 2015. This crowd-sourced website defines a mass shooting as any incident where four or more people are killed or injured by gunfire. The San Bernardino tragedy was one of three mass shootings attributed to Islamic terrorism in 2015, a figure far lower than the number of shootings involving domestic disputes or the number of accidental shootings by children. Still, many gun proponents used this tragedy as a clarion call to arms.

One such person was the president of Liberty University, Jerry Falwell Jr. Days after the San Bernardino attacks, Falwell told students at the evangelical institution known as a prominent platform for conservative politicians seeking higher office, "If more good people had concealed-carry permits, then we could end those Muslims before they walked in and killed them. . . . Let's teach them a lesson if they ever show up here." He then encouraged students to take Liberty's concealed-weapon permit course. To raucous applause Falwell affirmed what has become a truism among gun advocates in America: the best way to defeat bad people with guns is to arm good people with more guns.

Researchers at Harvard's T. H. Chan School of Public Health have likened death by gun violence in America to a public health crisis. When one considers both suicides and homicides, the numbers are alarming. According to the Gun Violence Archive, some 13,286 people died by firearms in 2015, and another 26,819 were injured. Children in the United States are 14 times more likely to die by gun violence than in any other developed nation. And the number of gun homicides in the United States is nearly 30 times that of the United Kingdom. This nation has what many feel has become an unsolvable problem. And despite memorable catchphrases and "good guys with guns" rhetoric, it is clear that the United States cannot arm its way out of this problem.

In confronting gun violence in the United States, I believe that we should identify and examine the problem at multiple yet interrelated levels. We can begin by acknowledging that the fascination with and fetishization of guns in the United States is not normal. There are roughly three hundred million privately held firearms in the country. When one considers the number of guns in the United States per one hundred residents (112.6), we have more than triple the numbers of France (31.2), Canada (30.8), and Germany (30.3). We are the most heavily armed citizenry on the planet. Many point to the Second Amendment as both source and justification for America's strong gun culture. Images of patriot militiamen from the Revolutionary War lionize well-armed patriots willing to die for liberty. Couple this with the western gunslinger archetype that rests in the popular imaginary, and it is difficult to distinguish gun culture from the larger myth of masculine, rugged individualism. We have all heard the talking points. Guns defend self-determination, protect freedom, and ward off government infringement. This is why, in the words of Harvard historian Jill Lepore, the United States can be thought of as "one nation under a gun." Firearms, not God, are viewed as the source of our freedom and protection.

If only this narrative were true. As much as we point to America's special relationship to guns, for much of this nation's history, the gun was anything but a natural outgrowth of "American freedom." As historian Pamela Haag argues in her book *The Gunning of America: Business and the Making of American Gun Culture*, guns did not become popular household items until the second half of the nineteenth century. This was largely a result of shrewd marketing at the hands of industrialists Samuel Colt and Oliver Winchester and the gun manufacturing companies they each created. Haag cites as an example how the Winchester Repeating Arms Company needed to boost slumping sales immediately following World War I. The company started a "boy plan" to convince communities that it was their moral responsibility to ensure that every boy between the ages of ten to sixteen had a gun. Throughout the twentieth century, gunmakers and subsequently gun lobbyists worked to establish a psychological and emotional connection between gun owners and their weapons.

This campaign worked for much of the twentieth century, as guns, masculinity, and sport were braided into a gendered American trinity. Yet when hunting began to decline beginning in the 1970s, gun manufacturers needed a new pitch. They found it in the narrative of self-defense.

Former marine Jeff Cooper's *Principles of Personal Defense* provides an instructive example. First published in 1972, this book went on to become part of the gun culture canon. It's advertised as a "timeless theory" and that "all free people who aspire to stay that way should read, study, and share the wisdom found within these pages." Cooper argues that because one never knows where trouble lurks, individuals must remain attentive and be prepared to act decisively. "The stake in personal defense is your life," Cooper contends. "You cannot afford to play by sporting rules. Be fast, not fair. Be 'off side' on the play. No referee will call it back." If potential threats lurk around every corner, then it is one's moral responsibility to fight back. The gun industry found its new marketing angle: fear.

Part of the tragedy of America's gun obsession is the way financial interests, cultures of fear, and mass shootings become mutually reinforcing. Despite violent crime in America being at an all-time low, the gun industry is thriving. After each mass shooting, gun companies report skyrocketing sales. FBI background checks in the month following the mass shooting at an Orlando nightclub that left fifty people dead were at 2.1 million. That is a 40 percent increase from that same month the previous year, when the FBI processed only about 1.5 million background checks. Mass shootings impel gun collectors to stock up.

I point to gun collectors specifically and intentionally here. What makes the high sales figures of guns curious is that fewer households in the United States own weapons. According to the General Social Survey out of the University of Chicago, about 32 percent of respondents live in homes that contain a firearm. This is down from about half of all households in the 1970s and '80s. This means that sales are being driven by fewer households that own an increasing number of firearms. People are literally stockpiling guns. Also, higher profits among gun manufacturers translates into increased financial investment in their chief defenders on Capitol Hill, the American gun lobby.

The efforts of the National Rifle Association (NRA), for instance, have proven wildly effective and sadly antidemocratic. Though repeated polls reveal that the majority of Americans desire stricter gun control legislation, the outsized influence of the gun lobby has led to just the opposite. Both state and federal governments have passed more liberal gun laws in recent years. In states like Texas and Georgia, the so-called "Stand Your Ground" laws allow concealed carry in spaces such as schools, bars, and churches. The NRA is turning the United States into a Hollywood version of the Wild West. Again, these laws are premised on the logic that the best way to defeat a "bad" guy with a gun is with a "good" guy with a gun.

Though such sophomoric clichés help manufacture desire and promote gun sales, recent tragedies expose the fallacy of this popular refrain. What does it mean, for instance, when armed black and brown bodies are not provided the split-second benefit of the doubt for being good? Ask the family of Alejandro Nieto. This San Francisco security guard and practicing Buddhist stopped in his lifelong yet gentrifying neighborhood for a meal on his way to work. A devout San Francisco 49ers fan, Nieto was wearing his brand-new team jacket, with his work-assigned Taser holstered at his side. A local dog walker called the police to report what appeared to him to be a "suspicious" Hispanic man. When four members of the San Francisco Police Department arrived at the scene, one officer reported on his radio that the situation had possible "gang involvement" due to Nieta's red 49ers jacket. Within minutes, the four officers shot a total of fifty-nine bullets at Nieto, striking him fifteen times in the head and chest.

Tragically, the case involving Nieto is anything but an isolated incident. Tamir Rice was a twelve-year old boy playing with a toy gun in a neighborhood park in Cleveland. A bystander called 911, though noting that what seemed threatening could very well be a child playing with a toy. Video cameras show that when police officers arrived at the scene, an officer jumped out and fired deadly shots into the child's body within two seconds.

Philando Castile, an African American cafeteria worker, was killed inside his car by a police officer in suburban Saint Paul, Minnesota. Castile, who kept a gun in his car with a licensed permit, shared this fact with the officer who pulled him over for an alleged broken taillight. This was the forty-sixth time that Castile had been pulled over by police in this same suburb over the course of a decade; according to an investigative report, only six of the forty-six times was Castile stopped for an infraction that officers could identify from outside of his car. By all accounts—including that of the officer who was later charged with manslaughter yet acquitted on all charges—when Castile reached for his license and registration in the glove compartment, the officer shot him dead. Incidentally, champions of the "right to carry" ranging from the NRA to Jerry Falwell Jr. did not offer a mumbling word in defense of Philando Castile. It seems that guns, even toy guns, in the hands of black and brown "good guys" only provides police officers with an instant defense: justifiable use of deadly physical force.

What does the church have to say? How might Scripture inform our moral response to this cultural dilemma? Jesus says in the Sermon on the Mount that the peacemakers are blessed. Moreover, Jesus encourages his followers to love their enemies and repeatedly chastises his disciples whenever they suggest or employ violence against those who attack them. Self-defense may be an accepted ethic in our world, but it is difficult to argue that it was acceptable to Jesus. In a world saturated by violence, he offers a competing vision of love and justice. In a world that both accepts and expects physical violence and bodily harm, Jesus' teaching encourages us to use the weapons of compassion, empathy, and mercy. In offering a contrasting vision of an alternative kingdom, Jesus invites us to imagine a kingdom of peace that runs counter to the normalized violence of our world. Thus Jesus invites us to act according to what we can imagine with our hearts rather than what we can see with our eyes. This is what it means to walk by faith, not by sight. Jesus, then, challenges us to confront convention and disrupt the status quo. Jesus' teachings challenge us to make "good trouble."

### Faith that Trumps Fear

In citing a desire to make "good trouble," I am citing the words of U.S. congressman and civil rights legend John Lewis. His entire life has been a battle against unjust laws and customs that deny life, liberty, and the pursuit of happiness to all citizens in the United States. In the process, he has endured vicious physical beatings and psychological terror that would rival the experiences of the apostle Paul.

In a commencement address given at Bates College in Lewiston, Maine, Lewis recounted how he first came to imagine a different way forward. Growing up near Troy, Alabama, at the height of segregation, he heard a repeated refrain from his mother regarding racial bigotry and segregation. "This is the way things are, son. So just keep your head down, and don't get in the way. Don't go causing no trouble."

Yet John Lewis knew there had to be another way. As early as the age of four, he began imagining a world free of Jim Crow. With his moral imagination, he could conceive of a country without racial segregation. Hence, when it came to evil and injustice, he desired to make trouble. This is what he now describes as making "good trouble."

What might this mean for us today as we consider the structural and physical violence of our world? On the one hand, we can just resign ourselves to things being the way they are. Like Jerry Falwell Jr. and other gun-toting evangelicals, we can attempt to fight violence with violence, bullets with bigger bullets. We can follow the examples of numerous civilians and police officers in recent years who have murdered unarmed citizens because they heeded Jeff Cooper's advice. They chose to act "fast not fair." On the other hand, we can live out the faith we profess. We can reflect the love of God we preach and sing about in the face of violence. Like Antoinette Tuff, we can live out our faith in the heat of life's tragic moments.

Antoinette Tuff served as a bookkeeper in a middle school in metropolitan Atlanta. One day, Michael Hill, a twenty-year-old white gunman, entered the African American school with an assault rifle and five hundred rounds of ammunition. Hill held up his rifle and declared, "We are all going to die today." Subsequently released 911 recordings include Tuff speaking in a comforting manner to the gunman. Her voice sounds calm, more like a trained crisis negotiator than a middle school bookkeeper: "It's going to be alright, Sweetie. I want you to know that I love you, okay? I'm proud of you. . . . We all go through something in life. You're going to be okay. It's going to be alright."

Tuff was speaking from experience. She has fought her own battles with depression and thoughts of suicide. At the time of this encounter, Tuff had just experienced a painful divorce and was battling financial difficulties that resulted in bankruptcy. A devout Christian, she had learned from her pastor that people of faith must always "anchor yourself in God." By this he meant making prayer a spiritual practice. Prayer is not something that we do at a designated hour but something that we live out in any given moment. This is what Tuff believes allowed her to remain calm on the outside though she was terrified on the inside. And this is what allowed her to talk to the would-be shooter, even as she prayed for the young man. Tuff was afraid. But her faith in God's love for all, even a crazed gunman, was stronger. If we are going to have the moral courage to make good trouble, we, like Antoinette Tuff, must be led by our faith, not by our fears.

## For Further Reading

Alexander, Michelle. *The New Jim Crow: Mass Incarceration in the Age of Color-blindness*. New York: New Press, 2012.

Green, Joel B., and Lee Martin McDonald, eds. *The World of the New Testament: Cultural, Social, and Historical Contexts*. Grand Rapids: Baker Academic, 2013.

Horsley, Richard A. *Bandits, Prophets, and Messiahs: Popular Movements at the Time of Jesus*. Harrisburg, PA: Trinity Press International, 1999.

Horsley, Richard A. *Jesus and the Powers: Conflict, Covenant, and the Hope of the Poor*. Minneapolis: Fortress Press, 2010.

Light, Caroline E. *Stand Your Ground: A History of America's Love Affair with Lethal Self-Defense*. Boston: Beacon Press, 2017.

Malina, Bruce J. *The New Testament World: Insights from Cultural Anthropology*. 3rd ed. Louisville, KY: Westminster John Knox Press, 2001.

Stern, Kaia. *Voices from American Prisons: Faith, Education, and Healing*. London: Routledge, 2015.

Stevenson, Bryan. *Just Mercy: A Story of Justice and Redemption*. New York: Spiegel & Grau, 2014.

Taylor, Mark Lewis. *The Executed God: The Way of the Cross in Lockdown America*. 2nd ed. Minneapolis: Fortress Press, 2015.

Tuff, Antoinette. *Prepared for a Purpose: The Inspiring True Story of How One Woman Saved an Atlanta School Under Siege*. Minneapolis: Bethany House, 2014

# 10

## Speaking Truth to Power

## A Subversive Gospel Ethic

> A country that tolerates evil means—evil manners, standards of ethics—for a generation, will be so poisoned that it never will have any good end.
> —Sinclair Lewis, *It Can't Happen Here*

> It costs you something to do good.
> —Zora Neale Hurston

### Taking Our Bible Back

The world has changed since that cold autumn evening when this book was conceived. Political and religious developments have heightened the questions and concerns of those six young adults. A bitterly divided country elected Donald J. Trump president of the United States. His ascendancy from reality television star to the White House has propelled several of the issues this group cared most about to the forefront of public dialogue: the rise of Christian fundamentalism, gender discrimination, and racial hatred are just a few.

When we met for dinner, many were concerned about negotiating the effects of conservative evangelicalism on their lives as progressive Christians. For some, it was how secular coworkers and colleagues viewed them as "holy rollers" for professing their love for the church. For others, it was the ways biblical literalists have established the rules regarding the "correct" way to read the Bible. To even suggest among many "believers" that one appreciates critical approaches to the Bible is enough to earn one the label of heretic. Despite these reservations, few would have thought that within a couple of years conservative evangelicals such as televangelist Paula White and Liberty University president Jerry Falwell Jr. would constitute the spiritual cabinet of the White House. The people my dinner party feared most now have influence at the highest level of political power

I am saddened but not surprised. One of the reasons that Donald Trump is in the White House is the overwhelming support of white conservative Christians. Over 80 percent of those who identify with this group cast their ballot for Trump. The candidate who quoted from "Two Corinthians" on the campaign trail and boasted of not needing to ever personally repent found common cause with a core constituency of American evangelicals. As a candidate, Trump promised to defund Planned Parenthood while asserting that women who have abortions should be punished. As president, he hopes to ban all transgender people from the armed services. And despite warnings from both European and Arab allies working toward peace in the Middle East, including Pope Francis, Trump formally recognized Jerusalem as the official capital of Israel. Interestingly, though both Jews and Muslims consider parts of Jerusalem sacred real estate—hence, the reason the international community has shied away from declaring Jerusalem the capital since the establishment of the modern State of Israel in 1948—Trump's decision placates many conservative evangelicals. They believe that Christ will ultimately return to Jerusalem, convert all of the remaining repentant Jews, and then reign over a thousand-year period of peace. The overt anti-Semitism among this wing of Christians

surely makes for strange bedfellows with some conservative
Jews. It's a classic case of theological and political interests
intersecting.

Aside from theological commitments, however, many still
find it curious that so-called values voters can support a president who flaunts his sexual dalliances and brags about sexual
assault. I do not. Some perverse biblical interpretations in this
book reveal that the leap between conservative-evangelical
family values and Trump's boorish attitude toward women is
not that far. When masculine honor is seen as having power
over and providing protection and provision for those under
male authority, men need women to accept a subordinate social
role. In the name of "biblical manhood," we reduce women to
backup dancers on our masculine main stages. Women become
the source of Adam's fall, not colaborers in the garden. They
are wives who tempt Job to sin, not those who embody radical
faith in the face of adversity. Our daughters are Lot's tokens of
sexual sacrifice, not victims of sexual assault. Women are pros-
titutes at a well, not the first to proclaim Jesus as Messiah and
risen Lord. And women are targets of Paul's condemnation,
not those who subsidized his ministry. These views represent
a critical mass of the Christian community. Tragically, they are
not any more enlightened than Trump judging women by the
size of their breasts or allowing radio host Howard Stern to
refer to his daughter as a "nice piece of ass."

So when Trump's opponent Hillary Clinton spoke of "shat-
tering the glass ceiling," it should not surprise us that many
conservative Christian women remained unmoved. Many
Christians view the glass ceiling not as a burden but as a sun-
roof designed by God. Through this lens of male authority,
women can benefit from the warming light of male provision
and protection without being exposed to the overwhelming
responsibilities of headship that God intended exclusively
for men. Thus, perverted yet prevailing interpretations of
common biblical stories provide a benevolent way of telling
women to "stay in their place." Male chauvinism and biblical

complementarianism are mutually enforcing reflections in the mirror of gender discrimination.

Unfortunately, as we have seen throughout this book, bigotry is like a virus that lingers at the crossroad of intersecting identities. It can easily plague all who do not conform to the cultural standard of power. Like purity politics, it was true in the ancient world and is true in our world. The same logic that condones the subordination of women translates easily into hierarchies of race. The same logic that privileges some people over others translates readily into marking certain religions as good or bad. This is how Donald Trump can frame Mexicans as criminals and rapists, refer to protesting African American football players as "sons of bitches," label those from Muslim countries as "radical Islamic terrorists," and describe the countries of Africa and Haiti as "shitholes." Yet when a group aligned with the alt-right movement and donning swastikas and Confederate flags marched through the streets of Charlottesville, Virginia, chanting "Jews will not replace us," Trump declared that there were "many fine people" within the group. Apparently, Trump did not want to offend white supremacists, who constitute a core of his political base.

I do not mean to suggest that all who voted for Donald Trump for president are white supremacists. Such a claim is as insulting as conservative radio provocateur Rush Limbaugh's claim that African Americans only supported Barack Obama because he was black. Nevertheless, white supremacists have made it clear that Trump inspires hope within their ranks. Participants at alt-right rallies chant "Heil Hitler" and " Heil Trump" with no intended disconnect. Young men marching in Charlottesville wore Trump's signature "Make America Great Again" hats while chanting "Blood and soil," a common chant of Germany's Nazi Party that connected ideas of white racial purity with claims to the land. And former Ku Klux Klan grand dragon David Duke offered his full-throated endorsement of Trump at a neo-Nazi rally: "We are going to take our country back. We are going to fulfill the promises of Donald Trump.

That's what we believed in. That's why we voted for Donald Trump because he said he's going to take our country back." Similar to Christian conservatives, in Trump white suprema- cists see a man who supports their xenophobic theological and political worldviews.

These are the reasons why I recommend the biblical reading strategies contained in this book with even greater earnestness than when my pen first touched paper. Our world needs more people of faith who read their Bible through a lens of love. As dis- cussed in part 1, this interpretive approach beckons us to enter the text and see as God sees. Who are the least, the left out, and the left behind? (Matt. 27) Who are the most vulnerable char- acters in the narrative? Who has the story rendered invisible? A lens of love keeps us from becoming enthralled with Abraham's authority and affluence. Instead, it asks us to understand Sarah's subordinate position and empathize with her anxieties as one vulnerable to male power (Gen. 20:2). A lens of love asks us to privilege the pain of Hagar, who was sexually exploited at the hands of both Abraham and Sarah (Gen. 16:5). And a lens of love asks us to view the world from an enslaved Onesimus's per- spective, not from the relatively privileged perch of Paul (Phi- lemon). In other words, this interpretive approach invites us to view biblical narratives from the underside of power to align with the most unprotected and defenseless.

To assume such a posture toward the narrative, it is imper- ative that we know something about the social relations and political dynamics that rests behind all Scripture. This is where the sociohistorical approach becomes particularly useful. It helps us interrogate the social and political worlds of both the text and the writers. Too often biblical literalists treat Scrip- ture as if it was not politically motivated insofar as sacred his- tory was never concerned with the distribution of resources and the securing of power. Nothing could be further from the truth. As I sought to demonstrate in part 2, sacred history was always concerned with social matters such as land distribu- tion, the appropriate forms of government, the changing role of the family in society, as well as political strife, corruption, conquest, exile, and empire. This is why we must interrogate how biblical writers responded to specific cultural patterns and social relations that may or may not be applicable in our world today. We cannot take the social world and cultural scripts of biblical writers for granted and chalk this up to a "biblical worldview." We ought no more privilege the cultural practices of the ancient world than we do our own.

The sociohistorical approach uproots and identifies all the things we took for granted and that still inform our world according to irrelevant and antiquated frameworks. As I recently heard New Testament scholar Cynthia Briggs Kittredge say at the Austin Presbyterian Theological Seminary Mid-Winter Lectures, "By moving politics to the foreground, we keep it from conducting mischief in the background." We pull from the background cultures of male honor and shame when reading the creation account of Adam and Eve. We draw from the background disputes over tribal affiliation and territorial disputes when reading xenophobic narratives of conquest and genocide. And we pull from the background how slavery in the Roman Empire shaped Paul's view of Christ's role in the world. In short, none of these specific cultures should be taken for granted when interpreting Scripture. They are essential to the interpretive process.

Finally, coupling a lens of love with the sociohistorical approach to Scripture provides us with a way to implement the prevailing ethic of the Gospels, subverting authority. This was our aim in part 3. Recall our way of viewing Jesus' miracle accounts. Jesus' acts of compassion flipped social relations by bringing into the center those whom cultural, religious, and political authority had pushed to the margins. The poor, the "unclean," dishonored women, those with skin diseases, and the mentally ill would all fail the purity-politics exam. These were the people Jesus embraced. Theirs were the narratives that the early Jesus movement and the Gospel writers shared with one another to capture the life and ministry of Jesus.

The same is true about Jesus' core teachings found in the Synoptic Gospels. Jesus inaugurates his ministry in Matthew with the Sermon on the Mount. It's the poor, those who mourn, the meek, and the merciful who shall inherit both the kingdom of God and the earth. In Mark, Jesus begins his public ministry in the synagogue by countering the sages, those traditional teachers of conventional wisdom. Then Jesus spends the entire evening healing those with infirmities. The Gospel of Luke records Jesus stepping into the temple and quoting from the book of Isaiah: "The spirit of the Lord is upon me." Thus, more than any other theme, the early Jesus movement emphasized how we treat the poor and marginalized in our society. "By this everyone will know that you are my disciples," Jesus said, "if you have love for one another" (John 13:35).

## Ending Religious Duplicity and Political Chicanery

Reading Scripture with love, extending compassion for the most vulnerable, and subverting authority are the central tenets of this book. This is why I remain so disillusioned with most public professions of Christian piety today. Rather than demonstrating any real concern with defending the defenseless or speaking the truth to the power structures of the gospel of challenging injustice, healing the brokenhearted, and liberating the imprisoned and oppressed, American Christianity has become a cesspool of personal piety toward individual gain. Rather than using a lens of love, too many read the Bible through a lens of power.

A lens of power interprets Scripture in such a way that it justifies abusive authority and reinforces social hierarchy. A lens of power privileges individual acquisition over altruism and personal comfort over compassion. A lens of power leads to gross distortions of the Bible, as evidenced in the perverse prosperity gospel or the Religious Right. The prosperity gospel baptizes crass materialism and hypermaterialism. It lifts the cross of suffering and sacrifice from our backs and turns it into a platinum pendant to adorn our necks. Rather than challenge economic injustice and inequality, the prosperity gospel sanctifies selfishness. Instead of understanding sacrifice as an act of love, the prosperity gospel sells sacrifice as a strategy of acquisition—you sow and you reap, and you name and you claim—as if God is running a cosmic Ponzi scheme. The Religious Right deems a political party as God-ordained and ideological talking points as Scripture. Jesus becomes a defender of free-market capitalism, small government, and tax cuts for the wealthy. Jesus opposes public and higher education in favor of homeschooling and provincial Christian colleges. And Jesus is a champion of unborn babies yet is ambivalent at best about social programs that feed those same babies once they are born. All the while, leaders of both the prosperity gospel and the Religious Right demonstrate a willingness to prostitute the teachings of Jesus for worldly possessions and political access.

A lens of love, however, challenges such religious duplicity and political chicanery. The method outlined in this book keeps us from cherry-picking texts that condone our selfish desires with decontextualized scriptural justification. It prevents us from using our faith to give cover to corruption while wagging the finger of condemnation toward the most vulnerable. A lens of love recalibrates our focus back to the teachings of the gospel. Jesus' ministry was one of love and compassion. Jesus' ministry, like that of the Hebrew prophets who informed him, subverted authority and questioned the status quo. It would only be appropriate, then, for us to interpret the Christian faith in this light. It would only be fitting to interpret Scripture with a lens of love.

# Glossary

**Etiology.** A type of sacred myth that attempts to explain how certain aspects of a society came into existence.

**Exegesis.** Derived from the Greek terms *ex* ("out of") and *hegeomai* ("to lead"), exegesis is a part of the hermeneutic process that involves extracting meaning out of a text based on several factors, such as original language, author, and intended audience.

**Hellenization.** The spread of Greek culture, religion, and language from the fourth century BCE to the turn of the millennium.

**Hermeneutics.** The wider discipline of biblical interpretation.

**Inerrancy of Scripture.** The belief that the Protestant Bible is without error.

**Magical realism.** Literary genre of narrative fiction that places the realms of the natural and supernatural in constant dialogue and that weaves together the mundane and the miraculous dimensions of life in a matter-of-fact style.

**Moral imagination.** An awakened creative consciousness that emboldens us to imagine beyond our present reality to see a more just and beautiful future.

**Narrative ethics**. An approach to moral development that focuses on the stories that inform how we ought to think, act, and interact with and judge others.

**Pentateuch**. A name given to the first five books of the Old Testament that is a combination of the Greek *penta* ("five") and *teukhos* ("scrolls").

**Rejection-replacement theology**. Based on a particular interpretation of Paul's letters and informed by supersessionism, rejection-replacement theology teaches that Paul rejected the "law" of Judaism and replaced it with the "grace" of Jesus Christ.

**Septuagint**. Greek translation of the Hebrew Bible whose name comes from the Latin *septuaginta* ("seventy"), abbreviated using the Roman numerals for seventy (LXX). Legend states that Egyptian ruler Ptolemy II sponsored the translation in the third century BCE and placed seventy Jewish scholars in individual rooms. Each scholar working independently came to the exact same wording of the Scripture.

**Sacred history**. A genre of storytelling and writing that transforms popular tales as well as actual recorded events into venerated histories.

**Seder**. A ritual feast marked by storytelling and prayers that marks the holiday of Passover when God intervened to deliver the Hebrews from bondage in Egypt.

**Sociohistorical approach**. Based on the belief that there is no text without context, the sociohistorical approach is part of the hermeneutic process insofar as it seeks to reveal the ancient world in which the Bible was produced by paying attention to social relations, power dynamics, and cultural scripts of the ancient world that always operate behind a text.

**Substitutionary atonement.** The belief that Jesus Christ died as a substitute for a sinful humanity when he was executed on the cross.

**Supersessionism.** A Christian theology promoting the belief that Jesus' inauguration of a new covenant means that followers of Jesus "supersede" the Jewish people as the covenant people of God.

**Synoptic Gospels.** The first three Gospels of Matthew, Mark, and Luke share a similar storyline and accounts. Scholars believe that the similarity in style is based on the fact that Matthew and Luke were derived from the earlier Gospel of Mark.

**Theodicy.** The aim to make sense of or justify God's goodness in light of contradictory evidence.

**Womanist theology.** A way of interpreting God's involvement in the world that pays particular attention to the experiences of women of African descent, as well as those of all minoritized women struggling against any combination of sexism, racism, and classism.

# Index